THE National ⚾ Pastime

A REVIEW OF BASEBALL HISTORY

M000086541

It's slipping by unnoticed, but 1993 is the 100th anniversary of modern baseball. A century ago this past April, pitchers for the first time in official play toed a slab sixty feet, six inches from the intersection of the foul lines. This was the last of the great changes made in the game during the vigorous, experimental, unrestrained, untraditional nineteenth century. The diamond was set.

A hundred years ago, baseball was already the national pastime, but it was still a relatively young sport. If we superimpose our year on 1893 and look back, baseball's development seems remarkably rapid. The game broke free from its town ball roots about the time Pesky held (or didn't hold) the ball and Slaughter scored from first. The great, professional Cincinnati Red Stockings took the field the year the Mets stunned everyone by winning a pennant *and* a World Series. The National League was founded in the year of Mark "The Bird" Fidrych. A walk counted as a hit just six years ago.

In 1893, a 50-year-old baseball fan had lived through the whole history of the "New York Game." Even youngsters of 30 had been able to watch the development of the sport into a business calculated to make money for "magnates," who three years before had crushed a player revolt and who now seemed determined to run the overlarge "big League" into the ground. They didn't of course. Outside forces, including Ban Johnson and an improved economy, would soon reinvigorate the game. (Our troubled sport could use another such jolt any time now.)

Sometime this season, maybe as you catch a few rays in the bleachers, or lie in a hammock tuning a lazy ear to a Sunday afternoon broadcast, or—best yet—perch on a grassy hill overlooking a high school game, give the game's past century a thought. And pass it on. Modern baseball is 100 years old.
—M.A.

THE NATIONAL PASTIME (ISSN 0734-6905, ISBN 0-910137-52-8), Number 13. Published by The Society for American Baseball Research, Inc., P.O. Box 93183, Cleveland, OH 44101. Postage paid at Birmingham, AL. Copyright 1993, The Society for American Baseball Research, Inc. All rights reserved. Reproduction in whole or in part without written permission is prohibited. Printed by EBSCO Media, Birmingham, AL.

Editor
Mark Alvarez

Designated Readers
Jack Kavanagh
Norman Macht
Robert L. Tiemann

For more than twenty years, the Society for American Baseball Research has published unique, insightful, entertaining literature. In addition to SABR's annual publications, Baseball Research Journal and The National Pastime, special issues have focused on specific aspects of baseball history. For further reading enjoyment, consider obtaining the SABR publications below.

PUBLICATIONS ORDER FORM

Baseball Research Journals
_____ 1975 (112 pp.) $3.00
_____ 1976 (128 pp.) $4.00
_____ 1977 (144 pp.) $4.00
_____ 1978 (160 pp.) $4.00
_____ 1979 (160 pp.) $5.00
_____ 1980 (180 pp.) $5.00
_____ 1981 (180 pp.) $5.00
  * 1982 (184 pp.) $5.00
  * 1983 (188 pp.) $5.00
_____ 1984 (88 pp.) $6.00
_____ 1985 (88 pp.) $6.00
_____ 1986 (88 pp.) $6.00
_____ 1987 (88 pp.) $6.00
_____ 1988 (88 pp.) $7.00
_____ 1989 (88 pp.) $8.00
_____ 1990 (96 pp.) $8.00
_____ 1991 (96 pp.) $8.00
_____ 1992 (96 pp.) $7.95

Baseball Historical Review
_____ 1981; Best of '72-'74
      Baseball Research Journals $6.00

Index to SABR Publications
_____ 1987 (58 pp.) $3.00
      The National Pastime,
      Baseball Research Journal,
      & SABR Review of Books

The Baseball Research Handbook
_____ 1987 (120 pp.) $6.00
      How to Do Research

The National Pastime
_____   #1: Fall, 1982 (88 pp.) $5.00
  *   #2: Fall, 1983 (88 pp.) $5.00
_____   #3: Spring, 1984 (88 pp.) $7.00
        19th Century Pictorial
_____   #4: Spring, 1985 (88 pp.) ...$6.00
_____   #5: Winter, 1985 (88 pp.) ...$6.00
_____   #6: Spring, 1986 (88 pp.) $8.00
        Dead Ball Era Pictorial
_____   #7: Winter, 1987 (88 pp.) ...$6.00
_____   #8: Spring, 1988 (80 pp.) $8.00
        Nap Lajoie Biography
  *   #9: 1989 (88 pp.) ....$ 8.00
        The Big Bang Era Pictorial
_____   #10: Fall, 1990 (88 pp.) $8.00
_____   #11: Fall, 1991 (88 pp.) $7.95
_____   #12: Summer, 1992 (96 pp.) .$7.95
        The International Pastime

19th Century Stars
_____ 1988 (144 pp.) $10.00
      Biographies of America's First Heroes
      (Non-Hall of Fame players)

Baseball in the 19th Century
_____ 1986; An Overview $2.00

The Federal League of 1914-15
_____ 1989 (64 pp.) $12.00
      Baseball's Third Major League

Award Voting
_____ 1988 (72 pp.) $7.00
      History & Listing of MVP, Rookie of
      the Year & Cy Young Awards

Cooperstown Corner
Columns from The Sporting News by Lee Allen
_____ 1990 (181 pp.) $10.00

SABR Review of Books
Articles of Baseball Literary Criticism
_____ Vol. I, 1986 ....$6.00
_____ Vol. II, 1987 (96 pp.) $6.00
_____ Vol. III, 1988 (104 pp.) $6.00
_____ Vol. IV, 1989 (128 pp.) $7.00
_____ Vol. V, 1990 (148 pp.) $7.00

Baseball in Cleveland
  *   1990 (40 pp.) $7.50

Baseball in New York
_____ 1991 (36 pp.) $5.00

St. Louis's Favorite Sport
_____ 1992 (64 pp.) $7.50

Minor League Baseball Stars
_____ Vol. I, 1978 (132 pp.) $5.00
      Year-by-year records of
      170 minor league greats
_____ Vol. II, 1984 ....$5.00
      20 managers and 180 more players
_____ Vol. III, 1992 ....$9.95
      250 players

Minor League History Journal
_____ 1991 (40 pp.) $6.00
      Stories and statistics

Run, Rabbit, Run
_____ 1991 (96 pp.) $9.95
      Tales of Walter "Rabbit" Maranville

Baseball: The Fan's Game (reprint)
_____ by Mickey Cochrane (189 pp.) $9.95

* = Out of Print.

SABR members receive Baseball Research Journal, The National Pastime, one or more special publications, membership directory, and The SABR Bulletin, SABR's monthly newsletter. Additional membership benefits include access to a national convention and regional meetings, research exchange and research paper collection, the SABR lending library, and nearly six thousand baseball enthusiasts like yourself around the country and the world. You are welcome to join any of SABR's 14 research committees.

To join SABR (membership dues are $35 U.S., $45 Canada & Mexico, $50 elsewhere) send check or money order (U.S. funds only) to: SABR, P.O. Box 93183, Cleveland, OH 44101.

SHIPPING & HANDLING

Please add $1.50 for 1 book, $2.50 for 2 or 3 books, and $5.00 when ordering 4 or 5 books. For more than 5 books, add $.50 per book. Ohio residents, add 7% sales tax. Foreign delivery, add an additional $1.00 in each category.

Make checks payable to:

**SABR, P.O. Box 93183
Cleveland, OH 44101.**

SHIP TO

Name _____

Address _____

City, State, ZIP _____

Before there was radio, there was...

The Board

Frank Keetz

It was the 1920 World Series. Cleveland versus Brooklyn. Opening game. Second inning. Joe Wood on third base, Joe Sewell on first base. Veteran catcher Steve O'Neill "slammed the ball down the third-base line" for a two-base hit which drove in Cleveland's second run on the Indians' march to a World Series title. Waiting for Brooklyn twirler Rube Marquard to take the mound again to pitch to the next batter, O'Neill scuffed at second base. It was at that moment, according to O'Neill's interview with H. C. Salsinger, veteran sports editor of the *Detroit News*, that he realized his greatest diamond thrill.

Back in Scranton, Pennsylvania over six thousand anxious fans were watching the huge play-by-play "boards" in front of the buildings of both the *Scranton Republican* and the *Scranton Times*. When the board operator put the name "O'Neill" beside the "At Bat" sign, cries of "C'mon, Steve" echoed through the crowd. Everyone was cheering for a local boy made good.

Steve O'Neill had been born and raised in Minooka, then a mining community a few miles from downtown Scranton. A miner at age 12, he and his friends, all of whom were wildly enthusiastic baseball followers as well as players, would take the street car from Minooka to Scranton to watch the World Series boards and dream of playing in the World Series. Now, at age 29, after more than a thousand games during eleven years as a minor and major league baseball catcher, Steve O'Neill's childhood dream had been realized.

Steve O'Neill

Frank Keetz, recently retired after 38 years as a high school teacher, just published a book about Schenectady, NY in the Eastern League during the 1950s.

A view from above 15th and Columbia, looking northwest toward home plate near 17th and Montgomery and the Wagner Free Institute, is the October 30, 1865 game, which the visiting Atlantics won 21–15. Twelve thousand spectators attended this contest.

Casway

Atlantics game attracted a huge crowd. Estimated at about 30,000 fans, this multitude forced the postponement of the scheduled game after one inning when the playing field was overrun by spectators. Two weeks later the game was rescheduled. This time only four thousand people were admitted, at $1 a head. But over 12,000 people witnessed the Athletics' 31–12 victory from wagons, trolleys, roof tops and unobstructed hills. Crowds like this disrupted life for the encroaching neighborhood. By the end of 1870, local property owners sold the ballfield out from under the Athletics baseball club.

With the creation of the new National Association of Professional Baseball Players in 1871, the Athletics moved to 25th and Jefferson and won the championship. The ballfield the Athletics took over was shadowed along the third base/Master Street side by the old grassed embankment of the Spring Garden Reservoir. But the facility and its playing grounds were in need of great repair. Wasting little time, the Athletics tore down the old grandstands and the encircling fence. They resodded and leveled the playing surface, erected a ten foot vertical slatted fence and constructed a pair of tiered infield pavilions that abutted near the original home plate at the 25th and Master intersection. Bleacher benches extended along the outfield lines.

The new Jefferson Street grounds had a capacity of 5,000. This figure frequently was doubled for major ball games, when fans lined the outfield fences and stood on boxes and unstable raised wooden planks. Those who could not gain admission purchased 25-cent roof-top seats or climbed a convenient overhanging tree. These trees were eventually taken down, but all calls for a centerfield pavilion fell on deaf ears. The club owners were too uncertain about the site's future and their profit margins to start any renovations. Even the advent of the National League in 1876 could not save the old ball field.

The Athletics opened the new league's first season at 25th and Jefferson, but suffering finances led to their ex-

pulsion when they could not embark on their final road trip. The old Jefferson Street grounds were left without an affiliated professional team. The Athletics' 1877 non-league schedule was the last season of games held on this site. At the end of that season it was obvious that more money could be made by turning the grounds over to residential developers.

It took the creation of the American Association, the new "beer ball league," in 1882 to revive the old Philadelphia Athletics and the Jefferson Street ballfield. Unfortunately, the original 25th Street site no longer existed and its remnant, a municipally-owned lot at 27th Street, was scheduled for a high school. As a result, the Athletics played their first Association season on a small renovated post-Civil War site, known as Oakdale Park at 12th and Huntington. These grounds, however, were too small to accommodate the city's only professional ball club. With a successful season behind them, the Athletics leased the still-vacant 27th and Jefferson Street location from the city.

On the northwest corner of 27th and Jefferson, the Athletics constructed the "handsomest ball ground in the country." The pitcher's mound of today's softball field approximates the April 1883 batter's box. This corner was backed up by a semi-circular two-tiered grandstand that later doubled as the main entrance. Painted white and adorned in "ornamented...fancy cornice work," the pavilion offered patrons armchair seating behind a wire-mesh screen. The structure was topped by thirty-two private season boxes, each holding five people, and a twenty-two person press box. A season ticket cost $15. The grandstands sat 2,200 people, but open benches along the outfield foul lines accommodated an additional 3,000 fans. After a successful 1883 championship season, the ballpark's capacity was increased to 15,000. Special features included a private external staircase for box ticket holders and a ladies' toilet room with a female attendant.

Attendance was supported by the Association's standard 25-cent admission fee and the ballfield's accessibility to public transportation. The grounds were five blocks from the 30th and Girard Pennsylvania Railroad Station and a few squares from the busy Ridge Avenue horse-trolley routes. Because of the state's "blue laws," Sunday games were played at the Gloucester Park grounds in New Jersey. A ferry from the South Street wharf took fans to this ball field.

The American Association Athletics played at 27th Street until the 1891 post-Players' League reorganization moved them to Forepaugh Park at Broad and Dauphin. This site belonged to their new owners, the Wagner brothers, who had become involved in baseball when they had invested in the defunct Philadelphia Players' League team. In 1892, the Wagners were forced to abandon the Athletics franchise, and were compensated with a team in Washington D.C. This withdrawal left both 27th and Jefferson and Broad and Dauphin without professional occupants. Only the National League's Philadelphia Phillies, playing in a grand wooden stadium on the southwest corner of Broad and Lehigh, remained.

The departure of the Athletics and the demise of the Jefferson Street complex did not dampen the city's enthu-siasm for baseball. Each summer, the Quaker City was preoccupied with amateur, semi-pro and regional professional leagues. Playing grounds, however, were now located along the new periphery of the expanding city. Prominent among these sporting sites was a facility at 52nd and Jefferson. Although baseball was not new to this neighborhood, it was not until the summer of 1896 that a sports park was constructed—the Pennsylvania Railroad and Y.M.C.A. Athletic Grounds. Over 12,000 loads of soil were carted to this site. A large grandstand holding 5,000 spectators was erected, together with a quarter-mile clay and cinder bike track. Tennis, croquet and cricket were among the other sports played at this facility. But these "Athletic Grounds" were never connected with any of the Philadelphia Athletic[s] baseball clubs. Even Connie Mack's 1901 revived American League Athletics had no association with 52nd Street. They played their first seven seasons on a converted industrial site at 29th and Columbia.

The ball grounds at 25th and Jefferson and 15th and Columbia are long gone, but they helped incubate the sport of baseball, and they deserve recognition as pioneering venues.

An 1884 view of the park at 27th and Jefferson, looking southeast toward 26th and Master

Casway

Jackie and the Juniors vs. Margaret and the Bloomers

Barbara Gregorich

On April 2, 1931, a 17-year-old southpaw for the minor league Chattanooga Lookouts faced the New York Yankees in an exhibition game. Before a packed Engel Stadium, Jackie Mitchell struck out Babe Ruth and Lou Gehrig as 4,000 fans thundered their approval. Mitchell then walked Tony Lazzeri and was pulled by manager Bert Niehoff. Despite Mitchell's heroics, the Yankees triumphed over the Lookouts, 14–4.

Mitchell's stay on the mound was a harbinger of her stay in the minor leagues: dreadfully short. Within two days Baseball Commissioner Landis voided Jackie's contract on the grounds that baseball was too strenuous for a woman. Jackie was devastated: she had hoped to pitch in a World Series and buy a roadster—not necessarily in that order.

Many a baseball fan knows the story. Few know that Mitchell continued to play baseball, and that the following month she pitched in Engel Stadium once again, before another sell-out crowd. Her opponents this time were also "Yorkers"—not the Yankees, but the New York Bloomer Girls. In this second game, Mitchell was again pitching for the Lookouts. Not the Class-AA Lookouts, but a group mustered from former and would-be minor leaguers—players who had no place to go because the Depression had reduced the number of minor league teams. Slapped together by Kid Elberfeld, the totality was dubbed the Junior Lookouts, or Lookout Juniors.

Norman Elberfeld had spent 17 years in the major leagues, starting with Philadelphia in 1898, but spending

most of his career with the New York Highlanders. A shortstop who occasionally played the hot corner, he compiled a lifetime batting average of .271. "Kid" was a shortened nickname, the full one being "The Tabasco Kid." Elberfeld's sizzling temper is revealed by the incident in which he and umpire Tim Hurst exchanged blows. Elberfeld had hit a long ball and slid into second safely, only to have Hurst, the home plate umpire, call the hit a foul ball. The Tobasco Kid got into such a furious argument with the umpire, repeatedly poking Hurst in the belly to make his point, that Hurst tore off his mask and smashed Elberfeld across the nose with it. Both player and umpire were suspended.

Elberfeld's last year in the majors, 1914, saw him a 39-year-old veteran. He is said to have mellowed, at least toward rookies—he went out of his way to give them tips and treat them well.

After retiring, the Kid opened a baseball camp in Atlanta. There, players such as Luke Appling honed their skills. Appling attended the Kid's camp in the spring of 1931 to improve his hitting, maybe both fair and foul. Although Jackie Mitchell claimed that Dazzy Vance taught her to pitch when she was six years old, she too attended the Kid's camp to improve her baseball skills. Mitchell was the school's first female graduate, and the Kid was proud of her.

With his newly-formed team of Lookout Juniors, Kid Elberfeld booked games throughout eastern Tennessee. Managed by the Kid, the Juniors played against town and semipro teams. As starting pitcher for practically every game, it was Jackie Mitchell who drew the crowds.

The Juniors' first opponent was Alcoa, a Tennessee town lying between Chattanooga and Knoxville. There,

---

Barbara Gregorich is the author of Women at Play: The Story of Women in Baseball, *Harcourt Brace.*

according to the paper, "batters were aiming for the fence, but with two away and a man on third, [Jackie] calmly fanned the strapping cleanup willow-wielder, who was swinging from his ankles and fouling them down the third base line like rifle shots."

Elberfeld's charges, as they were called, also won at Lenoir City.

With two victories, the Juniors headed home to face the Penn-Dixies, a top semipro team in the Chattanooga city league. In the first inning, Mitchell walked one. Two infield errors put two more runners on base, and a hit drove in two runs for the Penn-Dixies. But in the second and third innings, it was three up and three down as the Penn-Dixies faced Mitchell's one really good pitch. Described as "nasty" by some, "mean" by others, it was essentially a sinker. Although Jackie gave up one hit and two runs in the first inning, the Juniors blasted the Penn-Dixie pitching. By the eighth inning they were so far ahead that the 56-year old Kid put himself in as shortstop. When the dust had settled, the Penn-Dixies lay defeated, 12–5.

Next Jackie and the Juniors pulverized Rockwood, 34–6, as slugger Bill Wells, who would go on to the minors, hit his third and fourth homers.

Jackie and the Juniors took on all comers, winning a very high percentage of their games. The team was hot, and the news of its success spread to the North, where on Staten Island Margaret Nabel managed the barnstorming New York Bloomer Girls.

By 1931, Staten Island had been a hotbed of baseball activity for more than 60 years. In the early years, particularly the 1860s, the Island had been a cricket center, and was said to have the best cricket fields in the nation.

By 1900, the Island was turning out ships and baseball teams, often from the same dock. The Siscos, sponsored by the Staten Island Shipbuilding Company, were a top-notch semipro team, as were the Alaskas and the Fleet. In 1928, there were 250 baseball teams on the Island, one team for every square mile of land. During the 1920s and 1930s, major league teams—among them the Giants, Dodgers, and Cardinals—came to the Island to play exhibition games.

In 1910, three old-time local players—Dan Whalen, Eddie Manning, and Joe Manning, formed a team in Stapleton, naming it the New York Bloomer Girls. While the New York Bloomer Girls were late in getting started (bloomer teams had been around since 1892) they made up for it by lasting until the end of the bloomer era.

Briefly, bloomer girl teams were sexually integrated barnstormers, but most of the players were women. All bloomer teams carried at least one male player, the catcher. A few carried as many as five men. Rogers Hornsby and Smoky Joe Wood played on bloomer girl teams in their youth. Bloomers seldom played other bloomers: instead, they challenged men's town, semipro, or minor league teams.

When the New York Bloomer Girls were formed in 1910, Margaret Nabel was in eighth grade. She graduated from high school in 1914, having played baseball, field hockey, and tennis. It was after her graduation that she was asked by Pat Kelly, a catcher for the prominent Sisco Baseball Team, to pitch for the Siscos against the New York Bloomer Girls. Nabel accepted, but years later she recalled her relative lack of success that first outing: "I had poor Pat jumping all over the place, catching my slants, and the eight bases on balls I handed out sure do not speak well for my control in that game." Toward the end of that 1914 season, Nabel joined the New York Bloomer Girls.

While she continued as an occasional pitcher and out-fielder, and while she was a good hitter in the clutch, it was really as a manager that Nabel gained her fame. In 1920, before she was even 25 years old, she took over the New York Bloomer Girls as manager, and from then on the team was always referred to as "Margaret Nabel and the New York Bloomer Girls."

Throughout Staten Island and the other four boroughs of New York City, Nabel was well-known. By playing approximately 50 games a summer up and down the East Coast, from Nova Scotia to Florida, she became well known along the seaboard, also. She was, second to Maud Nelson, the most important person in bloomer baseball, providing women with a chance to play baseball one season...two...five...or, in the case of several players, fifteen years.

Nabel was very strict, tolerating no nonsense and exercising firm discipline. She had a keen eye for publicity and, as one man who played against her said, "wouldn't take crap from anybody." She was out to make a dollar with the team, and if she wasn't paid in advance of a game, she pulled the players off the field. Like many another barnstormer, she insisted that the playing field be fenced off to prevent freeloaders.

In 1921, her second season of managing, Nabel told a reporter that the New York Bloomer Girls, "use a male battery exclusively, as we feel that no female player can do justice to the pitcher's burden, and you will agree that the catching job belongs to a man, too." Thus Nabel usually fielded a team of seven women and two men.

Over the years, her philosophy on the necessity of a male battery changed, and several of the bloomer women, notably Helen Demarest and Ethel Condon, developed into pitchers. But Nabel never changed her opinion that women couldn't play in the minor leagues, let alone the majors.

When Jackie Mitchell fanned Ruth and Gehrig on April 2, 1931, it made news everywhere. In Staten Island, Margaret Nabel was asked to comment. On April 4, she responded. "A girl can develop a slow curve, an effective floater, good control, and perhaps everything else that a good male player can show except speed.... While I wish my Tennessee colleague every success, it seems it is just another publicity stunt."

A day or two later, when Nabel read in the paper that Jackie Mitchell's contract had been voided by Commissioner Landis, she offered the young southpaw a contract to pitch for the New York Bloomer Girls. Mitchell turned down the offer.

This either incensed Margaret Nabel or struck her as a golden opportunity. The New York Bloomer Girls, who had never before played in Tennessee, marched into the state and issued a challenge to the Juniors—a weekend game in Engel Stadium. Kid Elberfeld—himself no slouch when it came to making a baseball buck—immediately accepted and Saturday, May 30, was booked.

Perhaps Nabel intuitively sensed that Chattanooga fans, who had seen and heard about Jackie facing opposing male pitchers every day, would be more intrigued by the contest if the home-town hurler had to face a female pitcher. The newspapers loved this angle and played it up big, informing readers that Ethel Condon, 15-year-veteran second baseman and at the same time the Bloomers ace right-hander, was being rested for the big game against the Junior Lookouts. JACKIE HOPES TO ROUT PLAYERS OF HER OWN SEX, announced the headlines.

While the Chattanooga papers concentrated on Margaret Nabel and Ethel Condon, they didn't neglect the other Yorkers. A May 28 edition carried an article on Ginger Robinson. "One of the biggest drawing cards on the New York Bloomer Girls team is Ginger Robinson, a red-headed flash who patrols the hot corner. Ginger has long been known as one of the best girls in the baseball game. She picks up scorchers and pegs accurately to first and wields a wicked war club." And in the outfield, Nina "Babe" McCuttun was the team's slugger, good for seven to twelve home runs a year.

As anticipation built back in Chattanooga, Jackie and the Juniors mopped up eastern Tennessee and started in on the central part of the state. On May 25 they suffered a rare loss, to Tullahoma, 8–5, on a late-inning triple. Mitchell, possibly tiring, had given up three runs on three hits and two infield errors.

But three days later, as Chattanoogans were reading about Ginger Robinson, the Juniors were back in form, clobbering Sewanee 13–3, with Jackie surrendering only two singles.

Friday, May 29, the day before the game, the headlines declared, BLOOMER GIRLS HAVE BEST SLABBER READY FOR LOCALS. NEW YORK TEAM, WITH SPLENDID RECORD, HOPES TO CARRY JACKIE'S TEAM OVER THE FALLS.

Finally, Saturday, May 30: the day of reckoning, Chattanooga vs. Gotham. The game drew a sellout crowd of 4,000—the same number that had attended the Lookouts vs. Yankees game on April 2. Once again, the fans had come came to see the locals against the "invaders from the North."

Jackie Mitchell pitched three innings and held the Bloomers hitless, while her own Juniors got to Ethel Condon for one run in the first and one in the third. At the end of three, the score stood 2–0, Juniors.

Unlike Mitchell, Condon went the distance. In the fourth she was hammered for four runs while Stanfield, the Juniors pitcher, held the Bloomers off. In the bottom of the fifth, the Juniors scored another run, but then Condon settled down. With a man on third, Condon fanned slugger Bill Wells. The appreciative Lookout crowd rose to its feet in applause. And the fans applauded for Ginger Robinson when she leaped into the air and snared what looked like a sure base hit to keep the Juniors from scoring.

Stanfield, meanwhile, lost his control and began to walk the Bloomers, resulting in three Bloomer runs in the fifth. At the end of six innings, the score stood 7–3 for the home team.

The seventh and eighth innings were scoreless. In the top of the ninth, the Bloomers threatened, but managed to score only one run.

The line score shows that the Lookout Juniors scored seven runs on eleven hits and five Bloomer Girl errors. The Bloomers, on the other hand, scored four runs on two hits and three Lookout errors. This time, the South stood victorious, defeating the invading Yorkers 7–4.

After the big game, Jackie Mitchell continued to play with the Junior Lookouts until mid-July, when she left the team to pitch in the North. After she left, Elberfeld dissolved the Juniors and returned to his baseball camp. Bill Wells went on to play in the Nebraska State League. Other Lookout players returned to city semipro leagues. In 1933 Jackie Mitchell signed with the House of David. She pitched for the bearded ones for four years, then retired from baseball in 1937 at the age of 23.

After the memorable game, Margaret Nabel and the New York Bloomer Girls barnstormed their way back to the Eastern Seaboard. Within three years, Nabel would retire herself and her team. Not just this long-lived team, but all bloomer teams would cease to exist, replaced by softball players. With the ending of the bloomer era came the end of sexually integrated baseball teams—and the end of exciting encounters such as that between Jackie Mitchell and Margaret Nabel.

American League Diamond Stars Polished in Puerto Rico

Thomas E. Van Hyning

When Roberto Alomar drilled a ninth-inning Dennis Eckersley hummer into the right field bleachers to knot the score, 6–6, in game four of the 1992 American League Championship Series, it was yet another feather in the cap for the Puerto Rico Winter League. The oldest winter league in continuous operation completed its 55th season in 1992–93.

Alomar, Puerto Rico's top major league base stealer during 1992 with 49 swipes; AL batting champ Edgar Martinez; home run king Juan Gonzalez, and emerging superstar Carlos Baerga were four of the thirty junior circuit players born or raised in Puerto Rico. All thirty athletes have played in their island's Winter League.

Roberto Alomar played professionally in Puerto Rico during six winter seasons with the Caguas Criollos and Ponce Lions. He played under his father, Sandy, for Ponce in 1989–90 and also for Felipe Alou in his rookie season, 1985–86. Alou, the first Dominican major league manager, took the Caguas job at the request of the Montreal organization after Expos coach Larry Bearnarth was unable to answer the call.

Alomar on his father: "He told me the most important thing in baseball is discipline, but never forced me to play the sport...he provided good advice for the game of life."

The Toronto star had kind words for Montreal's Felipe Alou. "Alou is a straightforward guy much like Cito Gaston, who lets you play. He (Alou) gave me a chance to play regularly toward the end of the 1985–86 Puerto Rico

season and that was a boost for my career."

The following winter, Alomar showed his mettle by hitting .478 in Caguas' championship series win over Ponce as the Criollos won the title, four games to two. His RBI single off David Cone in game six gave Caguas a 4-3 lead and knocked the hurler out of the box in the fourth inning. Caguas won the game 9–3, but had to wait until 3 a.m. to celebrate. The contest was delayed by several rain storms and a power failure before being called in the sixth inning.

Caguas also won the 1987 Caribbean Series over teams from the Dominican Republic, Venezuela and Mexico. On Alomar's 19th birthday, February 5, 1987, Caguas lost a gut-wrenching 14–13 contest to the Dominican squad after committing eight errors and hitting eight homers. Bobby Bonilla, a reinforcement from the Mayaguez team, hit one homer for Caguas. Carmelo Martinez and Hedi Vargas had two homers apiece and Henry Cotto, German Rivera and Candy Maldonado chipped in with one each. After the 14–13 loss, Caguas executive Felix Millan replaced Tim Foli with Ramon Aviles as the manager, and the team went on a four-game win streak to cop the series hosted by Mexico.

Edgar Martinez, a cousin of major leaguer Carmelo Martinez, was signed to a Mariners' contract in Puerto Rico on December 19, 1982 by Marty Martinez, Seattle's third base coach in 1992, and former Expo Jose "Coco" Laboy. The soft-spoken Martinez attended American College in Puerto Rico prior to embarking on his professional career.

The 1992 AL batting champ (.343) is Puerto Rico's first one in the junior circuit. As four-time NL batting king Roberto Clemente did a generation earlier, he played with

Thomas E. Van Hyning is an assistant professor of Travel and Tourism at Keystone Junior College. He is the U. S. correspondent for the Puerto Rico Professional Baseball Hall of Fame.

and third base umpire Ziggy Sears ruled the ball fair and the Giants went wild. Magerkurth was the senior umpire and was at first base. The entire Giant team, except for those on the bench, surrounded the two umpires at home plate. Catcher Harry Danning and outfielder Joe Moore had been ejected, and as the argument continued, big George came down from first base to see if he could get the game going again. It was then that he and Jurges went at it. In his report to League President Ford Frick, Magerkurth said the fight was his fault as much as it was Jurges'. As a result both he and the shortstop were fined $150 and suspended for ten days. The Giants folded after that as the Reds went on to win the flag. (As a result of this incident, screens appeared on foul poles in all the ball parks in the major leagues—it would make the calls easier for umpires on balls hit close to the poles.)

On Sunday September 16, 1940, a famous incident occurred at Ebbets Field (see box). In a game with the Reds, the Dodgers had what appeared to be a routine double play. Second baseman Pete Coscarart dropped the ball at second. Umpire Bill Stewart called the runner out at second as he whirled to call the play at first (remember, three umpires were on the field) and did not see the ball drop. Magerkurth overruled Stewart and declared the runner safe at second. This did not please the crowd or Durocher, as the Reds went on to win the game and the pennant by a comfortable margin. The game would have been forgotten entirely except that, as Magerkurth was leaving the field, a short, fat 21-year-old pounced on him and the surprised umpire went down near home plate. A few punches were thrown before ump Stewart and park police pried the two apart. The umpire was not injured in the least except for his pride. As it turned out the "fan" was out on parole and the entire episode was nothing but a diversion. It seems the perpetrator had an accomplice in the stands who was picking pockets as the fans who stopped on their way out to watch the fracas were being fleeced. "Maje" dropped all charges against the parolee but the following season he was given police escorts from the field whenever he appeared at Ebbets Field.

That fall he was due to work the Reds–Tigers Series, but because Bill Klem was retiring, Frick asked him to step aside and let Klem go out working another Series. He was assured that he would be assigned to the Fall Classic in 1941. That wasn't to be.

The straw that broke the camel's back came on Thursday, September 18, 1941, in a game at Pittsburgh. With the Dodgers leading the Cardinals by two games on September 16, the long-awaited announcement had been made from the club office at 210 Montague Street—"The Dodgers are accepting orders for World Series tickets." Two days later, Brooklyn was leading 5–4 with relief ace Hugh Casey on the mound. With one out Pirate outfielder Vince DiMaggio hit a double and moved to third on an infield out. Al Lopez, onetime Dodger catcher, came to bat with the tying run just ninety feet away.

Casey went into his usual big windup and DiMaggio came running down the line about halfway. Casey hesitated in his delivery, and Magerkurth behind the plate yelled "Balk!" and waved in Vince with the tying run. Casey blew his top and bedlam prevailed in the Brooklyn dugout as Durocher came roaring out to the plate. In no time flat "Maje" gave Leo the heave-ho and play was resumed. Casey, who was furious, was throwing high and tight, and after the third ball Magerkurth asked Lopez, "Is he throwing at you or me?" The umpire then stormed out to the mound to talk to Casey. This brought Leo on the run again (although he'd been ejected, he must have been hiding in the runway). "Maje" once again threw out Durocher along with coach Chuck Dressen and pitcher Freddie Fitzsimmons, who was not in the game.

Lopez walked on the next pitch, then shortstop Alf Anderson tripled to right, sending in the winning run as the Pirates won, 6–5. Durocher went berserk. He broke all the lights in the runway leading to the clubhouse and threw a chair through the transom of the umpires' room. Several Dodgers were ganging up on Magerkurth on his way to the umps' quarters. "Maje" was a rough man in a brawl. One time in the '20s when Magerkurth was in the International League, he was attacked by five Baltimore players after a game. He KO'd all five and threw one of them through the clubhouse door! Even at the age of 53, he was set to take the Dodgers on, but umpires Stewart and Tom Dunn and some special cops restored order.

After being held out in 1940 to honor Klem, and in 1941 to humor Durocher, big George finally worked his third World Series in 1942. It was won by the Cardinals, who upset the Yankees in five games. He worked the first and fifth games behind the plate and there were no incidents, just good baseball. Things quieted down in Brooklyn during the war years. Magerkurth did make headlines coast to coast in the summer of 1945 when he knocked out a "fan" sitting in a box seat behind third base after a game in Cincinnati. The character had been heckling the official for two years and the ump just got fed up. The guy, who was over two hundred pounds, threatened to sue, but settled out of court when the umpire paid him $100 for medical expenses. The "fan" had been so annoying to the regular patrons who sat in that section, that they took up a collection and gave Magerkurth $150 for shutting the loud-mouth up! So the umpire made fifty bucks and was not fined by the league!

With Durocher being suspended for the 1947 season by Commissioner "Happy" Chandler and Burt Shotton replacing Leo as Brooklyn manager, "Maje" was assigned to work the World Series that fall between the Dodgers and Yankees (who won in seven games). Late that August "Maje" had suffered a broken knee cap when he was hit by a wild throw. He was out of action for several weeks. When the Series got underway the painful injury prevented him from standing too long, so he worked the foul lines—sitting in a chair!

After the Series the big umpire announced his retirement. It was the end of a great, colorful, and sometimes turbulent career. The first telegram he received said, "I'm sure going to miss you." It was signed—Leo Durocher.

"Maje" came back to New York once more to umpire an Old Timers game at Shea Stadium. It was 1964 and the Mets marked the 25th anniversary of the 1939 All Star Game by bringing back most of the participants. They introduced the players and then introduced "Maje". The great 75-year-old arbiter was cheered by the big crowd. He smiled and waved to them. Two years later, during the World Series on October 7, 1966, George Magerkurth died in a hospital in Rock Island, Illinois.

Magerkurth's famous battle had unexpected ramifications

—Jack Kavanagh

When the game ended several fans stalked the 6'3" Magerkurth, a hefty giant at over 200 pounds., and one tripped him. The umpire was flat on his back and his assailant, a stubby slugger, was astride him and viciously pummeled him. All this went on behind my back and was unseen for the same reason by those ushers ringing the diamond. The fight took place behind them while they faced the stands. It was another technique imported from Chicago [by Jack Haines, who had been brought from the Cubs by Larry MacPhail to oversee the usher corps at Ebbets Field]. It didn't make much sense to prohibit people in street shoes from crossing the diamond on the way to the center field exit gate after the players had been ripping it up with their spikes all afternoon. But it looked nice.

My own assignment when the game ended was to open a gate in the low fence that separated the downstairs reserved seat section from the rows of general admission seats farther back from the field. While I was doing this I heard noises that usually meant the blood lust of the crowd had been aroused. Whenever a fight breaks out in the stands at a ball game, people who have paid good money to see professionals compete climb on seats to watch a couple of amateurs maul each other. When I looked around I could see two men wrestling on the ground. One was an umpire. While I was sizing up this unlikely scene, I heard a deep-throated growl. A Neanderthal type was lumbering over rows of seats in my direction, grunting and shaking a ham-sized fist at me. I sensed that my green uniform identified me as "authority" and by some twist of a primitive intellect, this correlated with umpires and Magerkurth's decision. The beady eyes of the approaching beast glowed with hate. I did what any red-blooded usher would have done. I hurdled the rows of seats between me and the playing field.

Later I pretended I had been rushing to the aid of Magerkurth. Not so. He just happened to be where I was headed. My idea was to join the other ushers. They already formed two sides of a defensive square, although most of them were still blithely unaware that behind them an umpire was in a losing battle. A full-page picture of the huge Magerkurth being pummeled by a stumpy assailant sitting astride his stomach ran on the front page of the *New York Daily News* the next day. Behind them, an ushering colleague of mine, George Phillips, appeared to be gazing bemusedly at the fight scene.

Larry MacPhail was outraged, It was bad enough that his ushers hadn't intervened, the one whose picture was in the paper actually seemed to be enjoying the fight. When he arrived at the ballpark, Phillips was told not to bother putting on his uniform. Instead he was to report directly to Larry MacPhail so that the general manager could fire him personally. If we'd worn epaulets, MacPhail would have snipped them off Phillips' uniform and handed him a white feather for cowardice.

Soon Phillips was back and putting on his uniform. We crowded around as he buttoned the coat and straightened his hat. Then we saw his swollen and blackened eye. No, MacPhail hadn't done it. In fact, it saved Phillips' job. MacPhail, having been told the picture had been snapped just as the usher had turned to investigate what was happening behind him, assumed Phillips had been slugged in the following melee. Actually, Phillips had gotten the shiner hours after the game was over. He had been the second choice of a young lady he had offered to escort home from a bar. In stepping outside to settle the issue with his rival, Phillips had caught a roundhouse thrown by a different antagonist for a different purpose. However, he accepted MacPhail's interpretation and the assurance of future assignments of choice ushering locations that went with it.

From "A Dodger Boyhood," Jack's warm, amusing, and instructive memoir, first published in Baseball History.

games behind the Reds. The Grays won their next three games, but on July 22 they lost their second-best pitcher. Charlie Sweeney showed up hung over for a game against Philadelphia, then left the park midway through the game in a dispute with manager Frank Bancroft, who wanted him to play right field for the final innings. The Grays, forced to continue with only eight players, lost the game. Sweeney was promptly expelled from the club—and from the National League. The Grays briefly considered disbanding, but instead restored Radbourne to active duty and vowed to continue even if they had to banish everyone and field a team of amateurs.

Meanwhile, Blaine's campaigners had dug up information that Grover Cleveland, a lifelong bachelor, had in his younger days fathered an illegitimate child. On July 21, the day before Charlie Sweeney's desertion and expulsion, the Cleveland scandal broke into print in a Buffalo, N.Y., paper. Two Buffalo clergymen confirmed the story.

The Blaine forces savored this revelation about Cleveland's personal life, because there was no scandal in Cleveland's political record as mayor of Buffalo and governor of New York, while both Blaine and his running mate, John A. Logan of Illinois, suffered pasts tainted with political corruption. To the surprise of just about everyone, though, Cleveland admitted the charge. More than that, he wrote an article explaining the affair in detail, and was about to publish it when his campaign manager, Arthur P. Gorman, vetoed the idea—by throwing the article into the fire, according to one version of the story. The Republicans would make as much of the affair as they could anyway, Gorman reasoned; there was no need for Cleveland to aid them by dignifying their accusations with a detailed response.

Arthur Pue Gorman was a rising star in Democratic politics. A native of Maryland, he had spent fifteen of his formative years in nearby Washington, rising at the U.S. Senate from page to postmaster. In 1859, when he was twenty, he and two friends organized the National Base Ball Club, which fielded—by the time Gorman left Washington to become a federal tax collector in his home state—one of the top teams in the country. In 1867 Gorman became the first non-New Yorker to be elected president of the National Association of Base Ball Players, the game's governing body, and that summer accompanied the Nationals on part of the first tour ever by an Eastern team to the Midwest. After 1867, Gorman's formal connection with baseball gave way to his involvement in state Democratic politics. By the summer of 1884 he had been back in Washington three years as U. S. senator from Maryland. As it turned out, his contribution to Cleveland's campaign would prove as crucial as pitcher Radbourne's to the campaign of the Providence Grays.

From July 12 through the end of the month, New York's Mets had won fourteen games while losing only one, and although they led the American Association by only 2-1/2 games, their surge so impressed Met manager Jim Mutrie that he boasted his team could beat the best of the National League, too. When Mutrie issued his boast, the Providence Grays were in New York for a series with the city's National League Maroons. With Radbourne back in the box the Grays had just won four straight games, and on July 30 they held a half-game league lead of their own. They were so confident of ultimate success that they persuaded their manager Bancroft to challenge the Mets to a postseason series, "for a purse of $2,000," *The New York Times* reported on August 1, "each side to put up half." *The Sporting Life* on August 6 described Bancroft's challenge as a best-two-of-three series, and said "Mutrie accepts the challenge with the proviso that each club wins the championship of its association." (Details of the challenge varied with each telling. A week later *Sporting Life* described it as a three-game series with a purse of $3,000.)

But Bancroft had issued his challenge without consulting his bosses, and Providence club president Henry T. Root complained of his manager's action to National League president A. G. Mills. Mills had written to Root to express his disapproval of "playing for a stake," and had enclosed a copy of his letter to Henry Chadwick in which he echoed Chadwick's feeling that Bancroft's challenge lowered the league's dignity. Had Mills urged Root to withdraw the challenge, Root almost certainly would have done so, and the series would have been forgotten. But Mills knew that the challenge had originated with the Providence players, and worried that if club officials repudiated the series they might find it difficult to re-sign the players for the next season. He therefore urged Root to "employ all legitimate means" to keep the team together, and so the challenge stood.

Some have described the 1884 Providence–Metropolitan series as the first "official" World Series, but Mills' refusal to discourage it is the only sanction the series received from baseball officialdom. It was—like the first modern World Series in 1903—no more official than other inter-league exhibition games.

The Grays proved unstoppable. After losing on August 6 for the first time in two weeks, they embarked on their longest win streak of the season—twenty games (eighteen of them with Radbourne in the box)—to put the pennant all but out of Boston's reach. The Mets were finding it only a little more difficult to salt away the Association title, but prospects for a postseason series became clouded in disagreement. The *New York Times* reported on September 29 that the Mets had proposed a series of five games, "two in Providence, two in this city, and the choice of cities for the fifth to be tossed for, the winner in each game to take the total gate receipts." But Bancroft, writing to *The Sporting Life* three days later, rejected an earlier Mutrie offer and threatened to send his players home unless the Mets accepted his original three-game, winner-take-all proposal.

On the day the regular season ended, though, Mutrie

and Bancroft met in Philadelphia. Bancroft described the meeting in a letter dated October 16 and published the next day in the Providence *Evening Telegram:*

In response to a telegram from myself, Manager Mutrie came, last evening, and after a long argument we came to the agreement that the Providences and Metropolitans should play a series of three games on the Polo Grounds [then located north of New York's Central Park], October 23, 24 and 25, for the championship of America. The games are to be played under American [Association] rules, except the pitchers; they are to be allowed to pitch as they please; the winner of the series to fly a pennant next year as Champions of America.

Bancroft compromised on the financing: the clubs would share receipts and expenses. Gushed *The Sporting Life:*

These will probably be the greatest games ever played, and will be the first time in the history of the game that the champion teams of two associations have met in a formal series to decide superiority. If the weather is fine their meeting will be witnessed by larger crowds than have ever been seen on the Polo Grounds.

The Mets planned a gala torchlight parade for the eve of the series. This was the first time a New York club had won a professional league championship.

First, though, the Mets would play the fourth-place National League Maroons for New York's city champion-

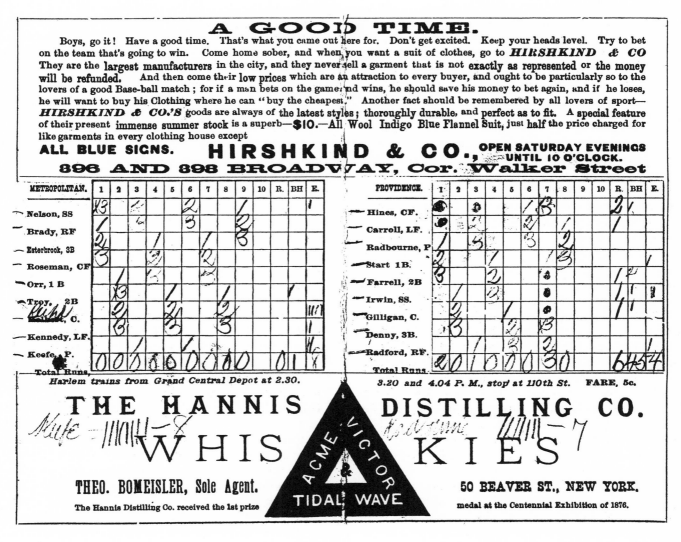

A scorecard from the first game of the 1884 World Series

ship. On October 16, the day Bancroft announced the dates for the Grays–Mets games, the Mets and Maroons began their three-game city series. The first game ended in a 5–5 tie, halted by darkness after five innings, and the Mets edged the Maroons 9–8 in six innings the next day. But the Maroons took a 2–1 lead in the second inning of Game Three, and held it until darkness ended the series after the fifth inning with the score 9–7 and the city championship unresolved in a tie.

For the Mets, things were to get worse. First, their parade was rained out, as an Indian summer day turned soggy. Then, the next day, their series for the championship of America began.

The literal rain stopped sometime after midnight, but figuratively it continued to rain on the Mets' parade for three more days as the team succumbed to Radbourne and Providence with distressing ease. In the half season that remained after his reinstatement on July 23, Radbourne had fashioned a record never to be paralleled in major league history. Before his suspension, his won–lost record stood at 24–8 (as such things are counted today; in 1884 pitching wins and losses were not officially calculated). This was a great record, but not spectacular. He had, after all, won forty-eight games the year before, when the season was fourteen games shorter. But from July 23 on, Radbourne pitched forty complete games (including *all* the Grays' games between August 21 and September 24)—winning thirty-five of them—and saving two other games in relief. It was in this half season that he earned the nickname by which he has been known ever after: Old Hoss.

The Mets' seasonal pitching chores had been evenly divided. Tim Keefe, like Radbourne a future Hall of Famer, enjoyed one of several fine seasons, with thirty-seven wins in fifty-eight games. For Jack Lynch, who pitched in fifty-four games and also won thirty-seven, 1884 was his only outstanding year. The Mets—unlike Providence, whose hitting ranked below the National League average—balanced pitching with offense. The official American Association statistics ranked Met third baseman Thomas "Dude" Esterbrook at the top of the Association in batting for 1884, and although research during the 1960s showed those stats to be in error, the batting leader who is now recognized was also a Met, rookie first baseman Dave Orr. In the Providence series, though, the Metropolitan bats proved no match for Radbourne's pitching. Only Esterbrook managed a hit for extra bases—a double in the final game.

The series was promoted only modestly, even by the low-key advertising practices of the day. There were ads in the New York papers, but they were no larger than ads for regular season games. No special scorecards were printed for the series. Instead, unsold scorecards from earlier games were recycled: blank slips of paper were pasted over the printed lineups and the cards were run through the presses again to print the names of the Met-

ropolitan and Providence players.

The rain that ruined the Mets' parade signaled a change in the weather that held series attendance below what the writers had predicted and the players had hoped for. On the afternoon before the start of the series the temperature in New York reached its high for the week, a balmy 76°. But just before six that evening, after several thousand marchers from amateur baseball clubs throughout the metropolitan area had gathered to form the Mets' parade, the rain began. By the time the storm ended seven hours later, nearly an inch of rain had fallen—and so had the temperature. By the three o'clock game time the next afternoon it stood at 51°—not wintery, but a sharp enough drop from the previous day to hold attendance to around 2,500. (Henry Chadwick, reporting the game in the Brooklyn *Eagle*, estimated the attendance at around 3,000.)

The Mets played the series opener at something of a disadvantage. Jack Lynch, who had been scheduled to pitch, was sidelined with a wrist injury, so Tim Keefe, who was himself (as Chadwick expressed it), "not in thorough winning form as regards health," took his place. Further, Bill Holbert, Keefe's regular catcher, was for some reason replaced at the last minute by Lynch's catcher, Charlie Reipschlager.

Keefe's wildness and Reipschlager's porous catching in the bottom of the first inning enabled Providence to score twice without a hit. Keefe hit the first two batters, putting them on base under the American Association rules. A pair of wild pitches, two passed balls and a ground out brought them around to score. Providence scored a third run in the third inning when center fielder Paul Hines singled and came around on another passed ball and two more wild pitches. Keefe then settled down to retire the next twelve men, but weakened again in the seventh inning, yielding four consecutive hits and three final Providence runs.

Radbourne, meanwhile, was all but invincible. After yielding a leadoff single in the second inning, he struck out six men in a row and retired twenty-two of the final twenty-four batters to face him. Keefe singled to start the ninth, but Rad got the next three batters on pop flies to finish with a two-hit shutout. Henry Chadwick observed that Radbourne's strikeouts were achieved by finesse rather than speed, and concluded his report for the *Eagle*: "The pitching of Radbourne was the feature of the game. His well disguised change of pace, his close watching of the batsmen to catch them out of form and his entire command of the ball were specially noteworthy points."

The "free list" was suspended for the second game ("cutting off the army of deadheads who usually throng the Polo grounds," one writer grumped), and as the temperature remained chilly, attendance dropped to about 1,000. Those who paid to get in, though, saw the best game of the series. Keefe's regular catcher, Holbert, was back, and perhaps Keefe was feeling better himself.

years. The Red Sox had one of the all-time great outfields, with Harry Hooper and Duffy Lewis flanking the incomparable Tris Speaker. This garden trio was outstanding both offensively and defensively, with Speaker second only to Ty Cobb among the all-around superstars of the 'teens. The Boston infield was well stocked with competent glove men. Larry Gardner was a standout at third, and veteran Heinie Wagner eventually passed the shortstop baton to the sensational rookie Deacon Everett Scott in 1914, and moved over to second base. Also during those years the Red Sox began to accumulate those deep arrays of pitching talent which led them to four pennants in seven years (1912–1918), with two second-place finishes.

Detroit's Tigers still recalled their three straight years of pennant glory (1907–1909), and were still paced by the most potent one-two batting punch in the league: Ty Cobb and Wahoo Sam Crawford. Cobb *always* won the batting crown and Crawford was almost always first or second in RBIs. In 1911, Cobb had hit .420, Crawford .378 (third in the league); in 1912, Cobb would hit .410, Crawford .325.

Cleveland's Indians were led by the aging Nap Lajoie, who could still hit and field with the best—.368 in 1912, .335 with a league-best fielding average in 1913—and a sensational rookie outfield talent, Shoeless Joe Jackson, who broke in with .408 in 1911 and added marks of .395 and .373 in the next two years.

Chicago, until then known for its pitching, still boasted the great Ed Walsh on the mound and was beginning to put together the nucleus of its later pennant-winning (though ill-starred) powerhouses. Buck Weaver arrived in 1912, Ray Schalk in 1913, Happy Oscar Felsch and (via trade) Eddie Collins in 1915.

By contrast with these talent-rich juggernauts, behold the starting eight regulars for Washington in 1912: four rookies, two sophomores, and two veterans in their fifth years as regulars—only one of whom even remotely approached stardom. This Cinderella Eight, which held together as the starting eight—starting most games at each position every year for four years—for longer than any other octet in baseball history, consisted of:

DAN MOELLER, rf—rookie, lifetime .243 hitter;

KID FOSTER, 3b—rookie, owner of the longest streak of homerless at-bats in major league history (3278 ABs without a homer!);

CLYDE MILAN, cf—the one established player of proven competence;

CHICK GANDIL, 1b—sophomore, and another genuinely good player, later to earn ill repute in the Black Sox scandal;

HANK SHANKS, lf—rookie, .253 lifetime average with no power;

RAY MORGAN, 2b—rookie, .254 lifetime without power;

GEORGE McBRIDE, ss—veteran .218 lifetime hitter,

though acknowledged a superb defensive shortstop;

JOHN HENRY, c—sophomore, .207 lifetime average with two career home runs (in almost 2000 at-bats). Actually, while Henry caught most games every year, the club deployed three catchers. Eddie Ainsmith, another sophomore, always handled Walter Johnson's starts. Third-stringer Biff Williams also saw substantial time behind the plate.

As is apparent, the hitting of this Murderers' Row was not a bit murderous. The club always ran well below the league average in both batting and slugging. During their four years together, none of the Cinderella Eight averaged over .300; only two averaged over .275. The highest one-year mark was Gandil's .318 in 1913, the second highest was Milan's .306 in 1912 (years when Cobb hit .390 and .410 respectively). Gandil's 81 RBIs in 1912 was much the highest RBI figure (Baker drove in 133 that year, Crawford and Lewis 109 apiece). Leadoff batter Dan Moeller's home run figures led the club: 6 in 1912, 5 in 1913. In 1915 no one on the team hit more than two roundtrippers.

Superb defense? Well, good, maybe. Milan was well-regarded as a center fielder; both shortstop McBride and third sacker Foster won praise for their glove work. But as a team their fielding average was barely above the league average. McBride was wide-ranging as well as sure-handed, handling more putouts and double plays than any other shortstop in the league in 1912 and topping all shortstops in fielding average all four years. But the editors of *Total Baseball* credit Washington with only fifth and fourth place finishes in their conglomerate defense stat, "Fielding Wins," during the 1912–1915 period.

Speed? Yes, these men could run. Milan topped the AL in stolen bases in 1912 and 1913, Moeller running second

George McBride

Clyde Milan

the latter year. All of the Cinderella Eight had steals in double figures in 1912, and all but one during each of the next three years.

In pitching may be found the club's one decisive strength—but that was concentrated in one magnificent man. Walter Johnson had his very best years from 1912 through 1915. Maybe no one was ever better. He led the league in wins each year but 1912 (when Boston's Smoky Joe Wood had his incredible career year 34–5). For those four years Johnson *averaged* 31 wins per year; the runner-up (Wood) averaged 17. In those years Johnson always led in strikeouts, averaging 243 per year; the runner-up (Cleveland's Willie Mitchell) ran more than 100 K's back, averaging 141. The Big Train averaged between eight and nine shutouts per year; the runner-up (Plank) averaged only four. Johnson's phenomenal strikeout totals were associated with remarkable control:

Year	Strikeouts	Walks
1912	303	76
1913	243	38
1914	225	74
1915	203	56

No, we didn't inadvertently omit a 1 or 2 in front of those walk totals. Johnson averaged fewer than two walks per nine innings, during years when he was the dominant fireballer and strikeout king of the league. (Nolan Ryan's walk totals during *his* strongest four-year strikeout period: 157, 162, 202, 132.)

But behind Johnson, the Washington staff was as nameless and talent-poor as the eight position players. Bob Groom had one excellent and one middling good year (24–13, 16–16) in an otherwise undistinguished career (120–150). In 1912, Long Tom Hughes was in the twilight of a productive career, managing 13 wins in 1912 before going 4–12 in 1913 and retiring in 1914. The others—men with names like Carl Cashion, Joe Boehling, Doc Ayers, Jim Shaw, Bert Gallia—were little noted and not long remembered.

It had been like this at Washington since the American League began. One *Baseball Magazine* scribe referred to Washington as the club "that had run eighth or seventh since Noah and the Ararat League were in full swing." In fact the franchise had finished sixth during the league's first two years (1901–02). But in the nine years beginning in 1903, Washington ran last four times, seventh five times, and lagged behind the league lead by as much as 55-1/2 games in 1904 and 56 games in 1909. The team *averaged* more than 40 games out of first place over the nine-year period.

From 1903 through 1910 the club never had a full-time .300 hitter; in 1911, perhaps as a harbinger of change, Milan batted a commendable .315, trailing the league-leading Cobb (.420) by a mere 105 points, while frequently-platooned 34-year-old Germany Schaefer, in his last full year, belted .334.

As the 1912 season approached, Washington fans had little to hope for. In *The Sporting Life*'s annual pre-season prognosis, Ban Johnson predicted a close race involving Philadelphia, Detroit, Boston, and Cleveland. Washington was last to be mentioned in Johnson's review, as he observed that "A big task has been assigned [new manager] Clark Griffith." *Baseball Magazine* praised Griffith's "shrewdness and cunning," but warned: "He will have no easy task in Washington."

On Opening Day 1912, as the front pages told of the great *Titanic* setting sail on its triumphal maiden voyage, the A's Coombs beat Johnson 4–2. In the second game, the apparently hapless Senators managed only one hit in a 3–1 loss.

But on April 15, as the fortunes of the great *Titanic* took their sensational dive, those of the Senators looked up. Johnson pitched them to their first win. Still, on May 30 the club lost the first game of a doubleheader and was mired in the second division with a 17–21 mark.

Then something happened. In one of the most amazing road trips ever, the no-account Cinderella Eight reeled off 16 wins in a row, "every game on foreign fields," as the *New York Times* put it. When they returned to their home city on June 18, President Taft, plus the Vice President, the Secretary of State, and a battalion of Senators and Congressmen, joined a cheering throng to watch a seventeenth straight victory, bringing the heroes to within

1-¹/₂ games of the front-running Red Sox.

Nor did their success end there. For the remainder of the season Washington's nobodies played 57–40 baseball, finishing second to Boston. They came in a game ahead of Philadelphia, even though the A's outscored them 779 to 698. They finished 22-¹/₂ games ahead of Detroit, though the Tigers also outscored them, with 720 runs.

Why were they winning? No single factor stood out, and *Baseball Magazine*'s F. C. Lane (the Bill James of 1912–1915) simply called the club "the crazy combination at Washington." A contemporary analysis by S. R. McDermott gave a lot of credit to the arrival of Gandil at first base, and to Griffith's management, but claimed that the biggest factor was the surge of confidence engendered by that seventeen-game streak:

> They became imbued with the spirit of success. They gained the confidence which comes from victory, and they continued to win. Once launched on their victorious career, once accustomed to the unfamiliar feel of victory, and they were not to be headed. They took all manner of chances on the base paths. They hit with vim and eagerness; their pitchers were assured of a gilt-edged support. They felt the confidence which comes from such support and the immediate memory of other victories. And they pitched like champions. There never was a more startling illustration of the power of a winning spurt than in the case of Washington.

Griffith himself admitted, "I suppose everyone was surprised" when his club began to win. The "Little Fox" (this was 1913—he became the Old Fox later) credited several items for the team's success: (1) "team play;" (2) "hustling ability;" (3) Johnson; and (4) his three "great, young

A young "Old Fox." Clark Griffith managing from the dugout.

catchers." Of the last-named, Griffith expressed the view:

> Given twirlers with some natural ability, the strength of a club lay not in its pitchers but in its catchers, for good catchers would make pitchers.

Probably the Cinderella Eight were a creature of their time, building success on steady, tight baseball, speed, opportunism, emphasizing finesse and cunning during the last pre-Ruthian decade, when such qualities could still produce a winning game. Foster, for example, though a .260s hitter with no power, was praised by a 1940 pundit as "in all probability the greatest hit-and-run batsman during baseball's first 100 years," and no less an authority than Babe Ruth himself (or one of his ghost writers) lauded Foster as the prime example of "great batters who are not .300 hitters." Milan was described in a contemporary account as "a serious thinking sort of ball player." McBride, "a brainy player" according to one writeup, and the infield's "headiest and steadiest performer" in another, later recalled, "'Course in those days you played for one or two runs, more than you do now."

Whatever the formula, it did not evaporate after 1912's heady success. In 1913 the Cinderella Eight again finished second, this time ahead of the mighty Red Sox (who outscored them 631 to 596) but trailing Philadelphia by 6-¹/₂ games.

In 1914 and 1915, they continued to play well over .500 ball, but slowly slipped to third and then fourth. By 1916, the team resumed its customary second division loser status. The Cinderella Eight broke up. Midnight came and the golden coach reverted to a rotten pumpkin. Reality returned to the banks of the Potomac.

But what a glorious dream was played for those four years, 1912–1915, by baseball's first Cinderellas.

The Goalie who Loved Baseball

Antonia Chambers

Charlie Gardiner was an All-Star NHL goalie, a Hall of Famer who led the Chicago Blackhawks to their first-ever Stanley Cup in 1934. But his first love was baseball. Before he went to the NHL, he played center field for the Tammany Tigers, a high level amateur team in Winnipeg who were champions of Manitoba in 1924. When he began playing professional hockey with the Winnipeg Maroons in December 1925, he lost his amateur card, but not his love of the game.

Six days before he died on June 13, 1934 at the age of 29 from a brain hemorrhage, he attended a game of the Winnipeg Maroons professional baseball (Northern League) team at Sherbourn Park. Though dying from uremic poisoning, a fact which he had kept to himself during the past year, he cheerfully mingled with the players before the game, and had his picture taken with two of them, Leroy Goldsworthy and Frank Piet. It was the last picture ever taken of him.

I came across this information in the course of my research for a book I wrote on Charlie Gardiner, tentatively titled *An Athlete Dying Young* (from the Housman poem), which I hope will soon find a publisher. Going through old Winnipeg newspapers for articles about his early hockey career, I found a reference to his participation in baseball, which piqued my curiosity. I eventually discovered that he played on the employees' team at Ashdowns Hardware in the Commercial League, and worked his way through the amateur ranks. In 1921, when he played for Norwood, they were Manitoba's junior baseball cham-

---

Antonia Chambers, a lawyer-turned-writer, is a contributor to the just-published Official NHL Stanley Cup Centennial Book *(McClelland & Stewart). Her book manuscript on Charlie Gardiner is currently being circulated for publication.*

Charlie Gardiner, hockey Hall-of-Famer,
as a Tammany Tiger, champions of Manitoba, in 1924.

pions. The next year, he played for the intermediate team, and as the leading base-stealer helped them win the city championship. Then he joined the Tammany Tigers senior team for the 1924 and 1925 seasons.

Years later when he was in the NHL, he told Chicago reporter Alfred Schoenfeld, "If I am a good goalie, then it's because I am fairly proficient at baseball." He loved the game and continued to follow it closely. In February 1934 baseball columnist Harold Burr interviewed him. Noting that baseball was Gardiner's first love, he said, "He would rather talk baseball than hockey." "Say," said Gardiner about his favorite team, "do you think the Giants are going to repeat?"

In June 1989, I, along with my husband, went to Winnipeg for nine days to conduct interviews and do on-the-scene research. At the Provincial Archives, I was thrilled to find several team pictures of Gardiner with the Tammany Tigers, as well as a photo of their ballfield, Wesley Park. But I was deeply disappointed to learn that the park no longer existed. I had very much wanted to go and see it, to stand on the field where he had played, and get a feeling for it. However, it had been torn down to build a college dorm. The hockey rinks where Gardiner had competed had met similar fates.

The third day we were there, I decided to look for Sargent Park, where he had played in the Commercial League. The odds were not great, I thought; after all, if the better-known arenas and parks had been built over, what hope was there for a minor field? We drove through the main district of Winnipeg, into an industrial area inter-spersed with the neat but inadequate homes of the working poor, much like the Winnipeg neighborhood of Charlie Gardiner's youth. We followed a city map, down Portage, right on Sherburn, left on Ellice Avenue, down Wall Street. Nothing. "Try the other direction," I said. We made a U-turn and went down Wall Street the other way. I was glued to the side window, but my hopes were dimming. "Stop the car!" I shouted, for there it was. Excitedly, we got out and walked over.

To a casual observer who knew not its history, the field would have made scant impression. A rust-aged fence cradled home plate, and a corroded gate was graced with an old-fashioned lock that no longer kept anyone out. Wooden benches once green had worn so smooth that they felt almost like stone to the touch. The basepaths were mottled with stones, and the plate, no longer there, had etched its memory deeply into the dirt.

But as we walked from home plate out to center field, I felt more than just the charm of the quaint or the fascination of sports history. It was like entering into a time warp. In my mind's eye I could see Charlie Gardiner as he "came tearing in, dove for the pill, grabbed it with his glove hand, and turned two somersaults but held onto the pill. A sensational one-handed diving catch..." just as the May 29, 1925 issue of the *Manitoba Free Press* had described. And as I walked back past home plate, I slipped a pebble from it into my pocket. Then facing center field one last time, I said goodbye to the unassuming park where a hockey hero had played the game he loved best.

Ehmke the almost-Vander Meer

In 1923, Boston's Howard Ehmke hurled a no-hitter against Philadelphia on September 7. In his next turn our days later, Yankee leadoff man Whitey Witt cracked a grounder to third baseman Howard Shanks. The ball bounded against Shanks' chest, and Witt was safe at first. Sportswriter Fred Lieb, acting as official scorer, scored it a hit. Ehmke retired the next 27 batters in order. The Lieb decision was widely criticised but was upheld by AL president Ban Johnson. Thus, Ehmke missed beating Johnny Vander Meer by 15 years in the consecutive no-hitter race. Actually, Ehmke's luck during his September 7 no-hitter was as good as it was bad four days later. A solid double to right by pitcher Slim Harriss was wiped out when Harriss failed to touch first, and a vicious liner to left field was mishandled by Mike Menosky and scored as an error.

—*Joe Murphy*

What was that about tools of ignorance?

Gus Sandberg, veteran catcher who has been with Los Angeles of the Pacific Coast League for the past several years, died on February 3 at Los Angeles, after being severely burned in a gasoline explosion. According to the police report, Sandberg had drained the gas out of his car and lit a match to see if it was empty, thus causing an explosion. —*from "Caught on the Fly," in* The Sporting News, *February 13, 1930.*

—*Dick Thompson*

A legendary meeting of legends

Satch vs. Josh

Larry Lester with John "Buck" O'Neil

About 50 years ago, two legends of baseball fame engaged in a battle of wits, a battle of brag, a battle of power.

In the 1942 Negro League World Series, a gentle giant from Georgia named Josh Gibson faced a slender, talkative traveler from Alabama named Satchel Paige. It was the high drama of a a great home run hitter against a famous fastball pitcher. Power against power. Legend against legend.

American folklore is made up of many legends, some based on fantasy and others on fact. In legend, there is John Henry, dying from the strain of racing a steam hammer, and the huge lumberjack, Paul Bunyan, and the benign children's favorite, Uncle Remus, spinning animal fables about Tar Baby, Br'er Rabbit, and other critters to a white boy on the plantation.

Away from the plantation, away from the timber land and the railroad yards, is the field of everyone's dream—the ball yard. Here, legends continue to grow. Remember the gimpy Dodger, Kirk Gibson, blasting the Athletics' Dennis Eckersley's pitch downtown in the '88 Series? Remember when the A's Reggie Jackson bit the dust after a lengthy diet of fastballs from Dodger Bob Welch in the '78 Series? Or the Series-winning homer by Pirates' Bill Mazeroski over the left-field wall, off Yankee Ralph Terry in the zany 1960 Series? Or, nine years earlier, the Giants' Bobby Thomson's global shot off Dodger Ralph Branca?

Larry Lester is the Research Director of the Negro Leagues Baseball Museum in Kansas City, MO. He is also the editor and publisher of the Museum's quarterly newsletter, Silhouettes. *John "Buck" O'Neil is chairman of the board of the Negro Leagues Baseball Museum, and a scout for the Kansas City Royals. He serves on the Baseball Hall of Fame's Veterans Committee*

But before all this, two legends materialized in the Negro Leagues: Josh Gibson and Satchel Paige. Josh was not your typical power hitter. The big burly catcher's stroke never resembled the sweeping swing of Babe Ruth, the over-striding swish of Frank Howard, or the 'twisted-fall-down' swipe by Reggie Jackson. Instead, Gibson employed a moderate stride, coupled with a compact swing, and violent wrist action. This ability allowed Gibson to be fooled by a pitch, adjust instantly and launch one out of the park. He seldom struck out, and he maintained a high batting average.

Now, Paige was unlike most successful pitchers; he didn't have a speedball like Nolan Ryan, a curveball like Camilo Pascual, or a darting slider like Bob Gibson. Instead, the lanky right-hander had a Long Tom (a super fastball), a microscopic Bee Ball (it looked about the size of a bee and hummed like one), a Bat Dodger (a slider), and of course a Little Tom (a "slooow" fastball). Satch was a pitcher with impeccable control and a hiccup windup that some fans called the "hesitation."

Josh was a jovial, kind, fun-loving man, but a serious ball player. Satch was boastful and unpredictable, but a brilliant pitcher with an infectious personality. Their images differ vastly, but their legends are equally mythical.

All-Star Jimmie Crutchfield, a former Crawfords teammate of Gibson, recalls a game they played one night in Canton, Ohio against the Nashville Elite Giants. "The Boston Braves had a farm team down there and it was all advertised everywhere about Josh Gibson. Boy, the park was crowded. The Boston Braves farm club had all come out in their team jackets to see the great Josh Gibson.

"Andy Porter was then pitching for the Elite Giants. And Candy Jim Taylor, the manager, said he finally got a

30   THE NATIONAL PASTIME

man who could get Josh out. Porter was a sidewinder, tall and lanky like Satchel. Anyway, [Manager Oscar] Charleston gave me the bunt signal and I squared off and took the pitch. On the next pitch, I singled to centerfield. Cool Papa [Bell] scored and I went to second on the throw to the plate. Josh then came up. Porter threw Josh something. Boy, did he hit it.

"I just stopped between second and third. I looked out to center field and the lights were shining through the trees. The ball just took off and then it looked like it just stopped! But it was still going, but it stopped and waved at us and took off again. Incredible!!"

Bill Veeck, owner of the St. Louis Browns, had this tale of Paige in a 1951 game: "Satchel had been called on for a ninth inning relief job against the Washington Senators. I told Satch to make it quick because the team had to leave by train in less than an hour.

"Paige then proceeded to strike out three Senators with only ten pitches. Afterwards, Satchel apologized to me. When they were boarding the train, Satch said, 'Sorry about that extra tenth pitch. But the umpire missed one!'"

Chet Brewer, former 30-game winner and teammate of Paige, recalls another Gibson story: "Once a young boy asked Josh if he could have one of his broken bats. 'Son,' replied the gentle Giant, 'I don't break bats, I wear them out. But I think I can find you one.'"

When he was fifty or so, Paige joined the Miami Marlins in the International League. In three years, Paige walked only 54 batters in 340 innings. One of his teammates, Whitey Herzog, in his book *White Rat*, recalls their time together with the Marlins:

"The Marlins once had a distance-throwing contest before a night game. [Don] Landrum and I had the best arms of any of the outfielders. We were out by the center field fence, throwing two-hoppers to the plate. Ol' Satch came out, didn't even warm up, and kind of flipped the ball sidearm. It went 400 feet on a dead line and hit the plate. I wouldn't believe it if I hadn't seen it."

Herzog recalls another Paige episode:

"We were on the road in Rochester one night, screwing around in the outfield. They had a hole in the outfield fence just barely big enough for a baseball to go through, and the deal was that any player who hit a ball through there on the fly would win $10,000. I started trying to throw the ball through the hole, just to see if I could do it. I bet I tried 150 or 200 times, but I couldn't do it, so I went back to the dugout.

"When Satch got to the park, I said 'Satch, I bet you can't throw the ball through that hole out there.' He looked out at it and said, 'Wild Child, do the ball fit in the hole?' 'Yeah, Satch,' I said, 'But not by much'.

"So the next night Satch showed up for batting practice. I took a few baseballs, went out to the outfield, and stepped off about 60 feet 6 inches, the distance to the mound from home. Satch ambled out, took the ball,

Paige and Gibson as teammates in the Dominican Republic.

brought it up to his eye like he was aiming it and let fire.

"I couldn't believe it. The ball hit the hole, rattled around, and dropped back out. He'd come that close, but I figured it was his best shot.

"Satch took another ball and drilled the hole dead center. The ball went right through, and I haven't seen it since."

Back in 1945, Sam Hairston, later a scout for the Chicago White Sox, had played against Gibson as a rookie. Hairston was a third baseman for the Indianapolis Clowns when he faced the Grays in Griffith Stadium in the nation's capital. "The game situation called for a possible bunt. And Josh was up. I don't know Josh from anybody else, so I breaks in for the bunt and Josh doesn't swing. Instead he steps out of the box when he sees me. He hollers at the manager, 'Hey, what are you trying to do, get this kid killed?' The manager looks at me and calls time and says, 'Get back, get back, get WAY back, on the edge of the grass.'

"I got back on the edge of the grass and Josh swings on the next pitch. I turned sideways just in time as the ball went right across my chest to the left field fence on one hop. If I had of been playing in, I would have been killed."

The feats of Gibson and Paige were often described with adjectives and superlatives—ignoring the facts and figures that are normally used to judge players. The two of them were real-life comic book heroes. They were black baseball's most treasured idols.

The living legends began their big showdown in the first game of the '42 World Series in Washington, D.C. It was the Kansas City Monarchs versus the Homestead Grays. In the opener, Paige pitched five shutout innings for the Monarchs, giving up two hits and striking out five before Jack Matchett threw goose eggs over the final four innings for an 8–0 victory. Third baseman Newt Allen led the attack with three of the thirteen hits off Grays pitcher

Roy Welmaker.

In the second game in Pittsburgh, Paige relieved the great Hilton Smith after six innings with a 2-0 lead. The Monarchs went ahead 5–0 before Paige gave up four runs in the bottom of the eighth. The Monarchs cushioned their one-run lead with three more runs in the top of the ninth. With an estimated crowd of 15,000 fans and the score 8–4, the stage was set for the duel.

There have been many versions of this celebrated contest between Josh and Satch. Some folks say the game was never played, while others claimed the duel never existed. Fact or Fiction? Real or Concocted? Truth or Fabrication? Listen to Buck O'Neil and decide for yourself.

John "Buck" O'Neil was the hard-hitting right-handed first baseman for the Monarchs that day. He later became the first black coach in the majors with the Chicago Cubs. "Buck" recreates the high drama of this grand encounter: "This friendly feud started when Satchel and Josh were playing on the powerhouse Pittsburgh Crawfords. With five future Hall of Famers, they may have been one of the best ball clubs ever assembled. Well, this was before the Pennsylvania Turnpike was built and we would have to go over the mountains to get out of Pittsburgh. When you got half way up through the mountains, they had places where you could pull off the road, so you could put water in your car or bus. The guys would pass the time by throwing rocks and stones down the mountain side, while the chauffeur was filling the radiator.

"Well, Josh and Satchel started talking. Satch said to Josh, 'You know, Josh, we're on the same team ... you never had a chance to hit against me and me pitch against you. But one of these days, we gonna be on different ballclubs and we gonna see what you can do against me and I against you.'

"Well, the day had finally arrived. We [the Monarchs] were not even thinking about Satchel's boast. This was the second game of the World Series. Now, we had won the first game over there in Washington, D.C. We are leading the ball game in the ninth inning with two outs. We had scored three insurance runs in the top of the ninth for an 8–4 lead. After pitching the first game, Satchel was weakening. He had given up four runs in the eighth inning.

"So in the ninth inning, their lead-off hitter, Jerry Benjamin, hits the ball down the third base line for a triple. Now, Satchel calls, (he called me Nancy), he said, 'Hey, Nancy, come here. You know what I fixin' to do?' I said, 'What Satch?' Now, we already got two outs. 'I gonna put Vic Harris on base.'

"Now I know the next batter is Howard Easterling, a pretty good hitter. Satch adds, 'And next I gonna put Easterling on. I wanna pitch to Josh with the bases jammed, I got something to prove.' I said, 'Aw, man! You GOT to be crazy.' Satch said, 'I don't know what you want to call it, but that's what I'm gonna do.' I cried, 'TIME!'

"So Frank Duncan, who was managing the ball club,

trotted out to the mound. I said, 'Frank! Skipper, listen here. I want you to talk to Satchel.' Then I said, 'Wait, I'll let Satchel tell you.' So Satchel tells Frank, 'We gonna put Harris on, then Easterling on and I gonna pitch to Josh.' Frank turns to me and says, 'I tell you what Buck, you see all these people here? They came out here to see Satchel pitch and so whatever Satchel wants to do, then let him do it.' So Satchel walks Harris. As he is throwing four balls to Easterling, he hollers to Josh in the on-deck circle. 'Hey Josh, do you remember the time when we were going over those mountains and we were playing on the same team and I told you what was going to happen some day?'

"Josh yelled, 'Yeah, Satchel, I know what you said.' Satch then said, 'Well Josh, this is the day to see who is the best! Now is the time!' Then Satch hollered, 'TIME!

'Jewbaby' Floyd was our trainer and he traveled all over the country with Satch. Wherever Satch would go, Jewbaby would follow. Jewbaby was like our team doctor. So after Satchel walked those guys, Jewbaby in his white doctor's coat and his black medicine bag marched out to the mound. Satchel had always had trouble with his stomach. Jewbaby opened his bag and mixed up some concoction, I imagine Alka Seltzer or something, in a cup and shook it up.

Now mind you, this was happening right there on the mound. Now everybody in the stands, KNOWS what's happening. Satchel had walked these two men and now the people are all standing, some 15,000 people. He took the cup from Jewbaby and drunk it down, right there on the mound, and gives the cup back to Jewbaby. He stretches out and gives out a loud belch that echoes throughout the ball park. So Jewbaby goes off the mound and now Satch is ready to pitch to Josh.

"Paige bent over slightly, letting both arms hang freely and wiggles his shoulders, to loosen up. He rises up and steps to the back of the mound and picks up the resin bag. He drops the bag to the ground and fingers the seams on the horsehide. And then looks straight at Josh and slams the ball into his glove.

"Satch said to Josh, 'I gonna throw you some fastballs. Nothing but fastballs.' Josh replies, 'Come on and throw 'em.' Satch counters, 'I'm not gonna trick you. I gonna throw you some fastballs right at your knees.'

"Satch wound up and tethered on one leg and fired. Josh didn't move his bat. Strike One! Satch bragged, 'Now I gonna throw you another one, but this one is gonna be just a little faster than that one, Josh.'

"Now I KNOW Josh can turn on a number one faster than anybody. So I watch Satch kick that leg up real high and BOOM, Strike Two! 'Now Josh I got two strikes on you.' But Satch said, 'Don't worry. I not gonna throw this smoke at your yoke, but a pea at your knee. Only it's gonna be faster than the last one.'

"The crowd grew silent, as Gibson steeled himself for the big pitch. Satch revved up, doubled pumped and threw Josh another Long Tom. Josh started and then froze, BOOM! Got him! Struck him out. Satchel looked like he got two inches taller, he straightened out, pulled his shoulders back and strutted off that mound. When he walked by me, he whispered, 'Nancy, nobody, but nobody, hits Satch's fastball.'"

Not even one of baseball's greatest hitters, on this day at least.

How do we know this colorful story isn't just a black version of the classic "Casey at the Bat" story? You know—there is no joy back at the old homestead in Pittsburgh, for mighty Josh has struck out. Fortunately, we know because, unlike fictional Mudville, Pittsburgh does exist and their *Sun-Telegraph* newspaper covered the game. And here's the official score sheet filled out by sportswriter Wendell Smith.

Negro League World Series
2nd Game—September 10, 1942—Pittsburgh's Forbes Field

GRAYS	AB	H	R	MONARCHS	AB	H	R
Benjamin, cf	5	3	0	Simms, lf	5	1	1
Harris, lf	5	1	0	Allen, 3b	2	0	0
Easterling, 3b, 2b	5	1	0	Cyrus, 3b	3	0	0
Gibson, c	4	0	0	Strong, rf	5	2	2
Leonard, 1b	4	1	1	W. Brown, cf	4	1	2
Bankhead, ss	4	1	1	Greene, c	5	3	3
R. Brown, rf	4	1	1	O'Neil, 1b	4	1	0
C. Will'ms, 2b	4	1	0	Serrell, 2b	4	3	0
x-Wilson, 3b	1	1	1	J. Williams, ss	4	2	0
xx-Whatley	1	0	0	H. Smith, p	3	0	0
Welmaker, p	0	0	0	Paige, p	2	0	0
Carter, p	0	0	0				
Partlow, p	3	2	0				
Wright, p	0	0	0				
Totals	**40**	**12**	**4**		**41**	**13**	**8**

x-Wilson batted for C. Williams in 8th
xx-Whatley batted for Wright in 8th

Monarchs   100 100 033 — 8 13 1
Grays   000 000 040 — 4 12 4

Errors: Sims, Benjamin, V. Harris, Bankhead (2). Two-base hits: Jesse Williams (2), Strong, Wilson. Three-base hits: Sewell, Benjamin. Stolen bases: Greene, J. Williams, O'Neil, Brown. First base on balls: off Partlow 1, off Smith 2, off Welmaker 3, Paige 2. Hit with pitched ball: By Smith (Leonard). Sacrifice bunts: Bankhead, Cyrus. Struck out: By Partlow 3, by Smith 2, by Paige 3, by Welmaker 1. Winning pitcher: Hilton Smith. Losing pitcher: Roy Partlow. Umpires: Craig, M. Harris and W. Harris.

Pittsburgh *Sun-Telegraph*, scoresheet by Wendell Smith, September 10, 1942.

	IP	K	W		IP	K	W	HP
Partlow	7.2	3	1	H. Smith	6	2	2	1
Wright	.1	0	0	Paige	3	3	2	
Welmaker	.1	1	3					
Carter	.2	0	0					

A History of Dodger Ownership

Andy McCue

The franchise now known as the Los Angeles Dodgers entered its 111th season in 1993. On the field, the team has provided a parade of well-known players and managers, 23 pennant winners and six World Series victories. Off the field, it has been associated with some of the most-recognized front office talent in the game's history. Names such as Charles Byrne, Charles Ebbets, Larry MacPhail, Branch Rickey, Buzzie Bavasi and Walter O'Malley have been posted on Dodger offices.

Yet, the standard works on the team are riddled with mistakes and misconceptions about who really owned the team, as opposed to who ran it. For, in all those 111 seasons, only once has one man owned the Dodgers completely, and then for only four and a half years.

The Dodgers began modestly, and in Manhattan. In the fall of 1882, George Taylor's doctor suggested he find a less stressful line of work. The 30-year-old Taylor was night city editor at the New York Herald. A baseball fan, Taylor decided he'd like to try his hand at running a team and he felt the New York area was ripe for one. There hadn't been a major league baseball team in New York since 1876.

Now, six seasons later, the National League was looking to get back into New York. And the league had been so successful that another group of entrepreneurs was considering a second major league, to be called the American Association. The Association also wanted a franchise in New York, giving Taylor two opportunities. Taylor's eyes focused on Brooklyn, where real estate for

a ballpark was less expensive, and where he hoped to take advantage of the city's reputation as the hotbed of baseball in the United States.

Byrne and the gamblers—Taylor's initial plans hit the rocks when his unidentified financial angel backed out, leaving Taylor with only a lease on some open land in Brooklyn. Taylor spoke to an attorney named John Brice and Brice mentioned Taylor's plans to a 39-year-old real estate agent named Charles H. Byrne, who shared Brice's office. Byrne was a former sports writer and, like Taylor, a graduate of St. Francis Xavier College.

Byrne's brother-in-law was Joseph J. Doyle, and the two men were partners in a gambling house on Ann Street in Manhattan. Doyle's investments in gambling were extensive. In those days before Kenesaw Mountain Landis, the relationship between baseball and professional gambling was strong. Only a few years before, several Louisville players had been expelled in the National League's first big gambling scandal, and Branch Rickey would later describe owners of the era as not far removed from "racketeers" and "ward politicians."

After investing $12,000 in equipping the team and grading the South Brooklyn site selected for the ballpark, Doyle paled at the cost of erecting a grandstand.[1] Nonetheless, he told Byrne to go ahead and work up plans, while he tried to raise more money. Doyle's gambling connections led him to the man who would be the franchise's financial mainstay for two decades.

Ferdinand A. Abell ran a casino in Narragansett, R.I. and had other business interests throughout the Northeast. When the team took out its incorporation papers in March, 1883, Abell's name was listed first among the

Andy McCue is the author of Baseball by the Books, *a SABR–Macmillan award winner in 1991. He is working on a biography of Walter O'Malley.*

partners, although Byrne was the president of the team.[2]

The exact ownership of the group is fuzzy. Neither *The Sporting News* nor *The Sporting Life* was being published when the team was formed, and the *New York Clipper* treated ownership as a matter of little concern. Most of what is known about ownership during this period comes from interviews done decades later and with at times conflicting details. In retrospect, it seems clear Abell and Doyle kicked in most of the money, Byrne a small amount of money and Taylor the lease. But Byrne, the team's president, and Taylor, its manager, were the men in the public eye, and Abell's importance was not clear to the public for almost a decade.

While Taylor was trying to round up financial backers, the National League and the American Association found their New York connections. Byrne's group eventually settled on joining the Interstate Association, a minor league operating mostly in New Jersey and Pennsylvania. They began play May 1, 1883.

The Dodgers were dressed in polka-dot stockings that first year and played on a site south of downtown, in Red Hook over toward the Gowanus Canal. Washington Park was in a working class, Irish neighborhood, well served by trolley and street car lines.

As president, Byrne performed all the jobs a team's front office staff would do today. He supervised tickets, concessions, ballpark acquisition and maintenance, duties he sometimes delegated to a young employee named Charles Hercules Ebbets, who joined the club May 12, 1883, the day of its first game at Washington Park. In addition, Byrne had significant input on trades and purchases, a job he shared with the team's manager.

Byrne was a small man, a Napoleon to his admirers. *The Sporting Life* described him as "a nervous little man, full of life and grit, a good talker, very earnest and aggressive..."[3] Byrne was to grow into one of the most influential voices in the American Association and, later, the National League.

Major League—But for the moment, he was leading a team which was going nowhere in the Interstate Association until the league-leading Merritts of Camden, N.J. folded in July. Byrne snapped up five of their best players and Brooklyn surged to the pennant. Flushed with this success, Byrne talked his way into the American Association for the 1884 season, abandoning the polka-dot stockings, which didn't wear well, and eventually turning to Wanamaker's for the team's uniforms.[4]

In the Association, Byrne's team was clearly outclassed, falling to ninth place in a 12-team league that year. Taylor was replaced as manager before the 1885 season, and left the partnership around the same time.[5] Abell and his money took a more prominent role in the team. Byrne scooped several players out of the National League's Cleveland franchise when it collapsed. He picked up more from the American Association's original New York Mets when that team folded after the 1887 season, and he bought the contracts of other AA stars: Bob Caruthers, Dave Foutz, Oyster Burns, and Hub Collins. By 1889, Byrne's strengthened team won the American Association pennant.

But more financial strains, and consequent changes in ownership, were on the horizon.

In 1890, Byrne moved the Dodgers into the National League. Brooklyn's ascension was by no means smooth. The winter of 1889-90 saw the formation of the Players' League. The Players' League had grown out of the Brotherhood of Professional Base Ball Players, a union dedicated to higher salaries and greater freedom of movement for players.

That winter, the players finished lining up their own magnates, as team owners were called well into the next century. Several were street car tycoons. Brooklyn's Players' League entry was bankrolled by George W. Chauncey, the wealthy scion of a prominent Brooklyn family with extensive real estate interests. His front man was Wendell Goodwin, a street car executive who served as president of the Brooklyn Players' League club.

With the financiers lined up, the Players' League clubs looked to make the Brotherhood's dreams come true with the offer of higher salaries for players to jump leagues. They did. Several National League teams, especially the champion Giants, were devastated. They lost seven of their eight everyday players and all but one of their top pitchers. There were 21 future Hall of Fame members who played in the majors in both 1889 and 1890, and 13 of them moved to the Players' League.

Byrne would also have more financial competition. The New York metropolis would boast five major league teams in 1890. Brooklyn and New York had teams in both the National League and the Players' League. The American Association had also cobbled together a Brooklyn team. Faced with the competition, Byrne felt that all he could do was meet Players' League offers.

NL pennant—It was to be his salvation. With the 1889 American Association pennant-winning lineup virtually intact, Brooklyn swept to the National League flag in 1890. The victory enabled Byrne's team to lose less money, $25,000, than any of the other New York teams. It also left Byrne's group in a strong position when the Players' League magnates began to sell out the Brotherhood that winter.

Chauncey and his fellow Brooklyn Brotherhood owners had more ready cash, but that was their only asset. Byrne's group had the franchise in the more stable league, the better players and the better prospects.

Eventually, the deal was cut. The Chauncey group agreed to pay Abell, Byrne and Doyle $30,000 in cash and to give them another $10,000 out of future profits. This implied a value for the franchise of approximately $80,000, although it was capitalized at $250,000. A new corporation was created, with Abell, Byrne and Doyle controlling 50.4 percent of the shares initially. Byrne remained as president and three of the five directors slots went to this triumvirate. Chauncey's group got the other two seats on the board and the remainder of the stock. The Players' League group also got its manager, John Montgomery Ward, named to replace Bill McGunnigle despite his two straight pennants. In addition, Chauncey won the transfer of the Dodgers to Eastern Park on land he owned in the East New York section of Brooklyn, land served by trolley lines in which other members of the Chauncey group owned interests.[6]

For Chauncey and his partners in the trolley business and real estate, the move to East New York was presumably good business. For the Dodgers, it definitely was not. As if setting a pattern for Dodger ownership for the next quarter century, the Players' League group didn't fulfill its part of the merger agreement. They paid only $22,000 of the $30,000 cash, and then began ceding stock to Abell and Byrne.[7] When baseball profits weren't forthcoming in subsequent years, they ceded more stock to Abell rather than come up with the unpaid balance. Over the next few years, several smaller members of the Players' League group would sell out to Abell.

Abell's dominance was also cemented by the withdrawal of Doyle from the partnership. Doyle's previously close relationship with Abell had deteriorated over the years. Ebbets said Doyle was frustrated by the poor attendance caused by Eastern Park's location, even though the Dodgers were the reigning National League champions. Doyle wanted out and came up with an offer from two men *The Sporting News* identified only by their last names, Marx and Jolly, and their occupation, gamblers.[8]

Abell, the casino operator, said he was dismayed at the idea of gambling men coming into baseball. More believably, he also was reported to be worried Doyle would convince his highly esteemed brother-in-law, Byrne, to go with him and start another American Association team in Brooklyn. Through Chauncey's man Goodwin, Abell convinced Doyle to sell out to him in January 1892. Byrne also sold some shares to Abell during the early 1890s.

Charles Ebbets and tough times—These years perhaps also saw the first appearance of the name Charles Ebbets on the rolls of the franchise's owners. Chauncey reportedly took a shine to Ebbets and sold him a small piece of his own shares.[9] It must have been a very small piece. By the mid-1890s, Abell told a reporter, he owned 51 percent of the team, Byrne 12 percent, and the Chauncey group 37 percent.[10]

The Gay '90s weren't for the Brooklyn team. Attendance, which had hit 353,690 in 1889, averaged 184,000 during the 1890s. Ebbets, in later years, made it clear he thought the major problem was the location.[11] East New York was just too far for most people. The mediocre quality of the team didn't help much either.

The team lost money virtually every year. Appeals were made to the shareholders to make up the deficits, but only Abell responded. Ebbets called him "the human war chest."[12] The Rhode Island financier slowly hiked his share of the team. It wasn't as if he wanted to. Abell had a standing offer to his partners that he would either buy them out or sell to them, but only a few of the smaller investors took up his offer, and then only to sell out. By 1897, Abell said, he had lost $100,000 on his investment in the team. Almost all of the losses had occurred beginning with the Players' League competition, but he had lost $25,000 in the 1896 and 1897 seasons alone. Charles Ebbets saw his chance.

Born in Manhattan's Greenwich Village on October 29, 1859, Charles Ebbets had begun working for the team at its first home game in the Interstate Association, printing and selling scorecards. He had left school early, joining an architectural firm where he worked as a draftsman on the Metropolitan Hotel and Niblo's Garden, a famous amusement center. He later went to work for publishing houses, selling cheap fiction and keeping the books. All these skills were to stand him in good stead when he ran the Dodgers, building Ebbets Field, overseeing marketing and keeping track of the books. At first, Ebbets was a glorified office boy, doing whatever Byrne needed done. Soon, Byrne was delegating substantial tasks, beginning with scheduling.

Ebbets developed a reputation as cheap. Perhaps this was simply because he was among the first of baseball team owners to build up a considerable fortune solely through the game, and without having been a player. But it's also because he *was* cheap. One day, a reporter found him arguing with the woman who washed the Dodgers' uniforms. "You want to make a living. If I pay what you want for washing these uniforms, I can't possibly make a living," Ebbets was yelling.

During games, Ebbets' customary perch was a high-backed accountant's stool behind home plate. He was accessible to the fans and his reputation for cheapness, emphasized by the newspapers, was a constant source of banter. During one high-volume conversation, Ebbets felt compelled to point out to his debating partner that he was the only major league owner who didn't have a car.[13]

He did have an appetite. Abe Yager, sports editor of the *Brooklyn Eagle*, told of attending a 13-course World Series banquet one evening at the Waldorf with Ebbets and some other writers. After the banquet, Ebbets and his party went downstairs to the hotel's bar and Ebbets washed down a plate of hors d'oeuvres with beer. Then they decided to walk down to Nick Engel's bar, a favorite with the sports crowd. Engel's bar was about 20 blocks south of the hotel and every block, it seemed, had a tavern. Ebbets led Yager and the sportswriters into each tavern where he sampled the free lunch traditional at bars of the period. When they finally made it to Engel's, Ebbets polished off a couple of dozen raw oysters.[14]

Ebbets' reputation wasn't all negative, for baseball was his business, unlike owners who could be distracted by producing musicals, or running breweries or ice-making companies. He brought some original thought to the game. He was the first to suggest scheduled times for batting and fielding practice before games.[15]

Ebbets was a joiner, for he took his marketing responsibilities seriously. He was active in the Masons, bowling, bicycling, and Democratic Party politics. He had been elected a State Assemblyman and an alderman, and had lost an 1897 race for city councilman by literally the narrowest of margins, 23,183 votes to 23,182. He also lost a 1904 race for the State Senate when Democrats were buried in the Theodore Roosevelt landslide.

With the Dodgers' losses mounting in late 1897, Ebbets made his move. He arranged to borrow money to buy the Chauncey group's shares. The reported purchase price of $25,000 implied a value of between $75,000 and $100,000 for the whole team.[16] He then secured an option on Abell's shares. On January 1, 1898, he invited the reporters who covered the Brooklyn team to a dinner and announced that he now controlled eighty-five percent of the team. The remaining shares were owned by Byrne, who was on his deathbed. On January 4, the man who had run the team since it had been founded fifteen years before, died.

The results for Ebbets were mixed. On the positive side, he quickly assumed Byrne's role. With Abell's backing, he was elected president. As had Byrne, he would exercise control over the team until his own death in 1925, while his stable of financial backers and partners changed several times.

But he didn't gain ownership. He didn't come anywhere near it. His option to buy Abell's shares ran out Feb. 1 and Ebbets conceded he hadn't been able to raise the money. Abell decided not to sell out to anyone else.

What happened to Ebbets' purchase of the Chauncey shares isn't clear, but what is clear is that by the next winter Ebbets owned only eighteen percent of the team, so presumably Abell picked up some of these shares as well.

However, Ebbets' management was already bearing fruit. He moved the team back from Eastern Park to a location diagonally across the intersection from the old Washington Park in the Red Hook section of South Brooklyn. It was a location which proved much more convenient for fans. Ebbets' problem was finding $25,000 to build a new facility. He'd hocked himself to buy out the old Players' League magnates and Abell was reluctant to sink any more money.

His white knights were the trolley car magnates, including Al Johnson, once president of the Players' League. Johnson's Nassau Railroad and the Brooklyn Heights Railroad companies bought the site, graded it and built what became known as the New Washington Park for about $15,000. In addition, they agreed to charge only $5,000 in annual rent, $2,500 less than the team had paid at Eastern Park.[17]

Syndicate baseball—But Ebbets also needed a better club than the one that had finished a dismal tenth in 1898. He saw the potential for what was then called syndicate baseball. Essentially, syndicate ownership was control of more than one team by one management group. The owners would then move all the best players to the team in the better market, leaving the other team to languish.

Ebbets and Abell got in touch with Harry Von der Horst. Von der Horst was a Baltimore brewer who had owned the Orioles since they had been in the American Association with Byrne's teams. But even in the early and mid-1890s, when the Orioles were winning National League pennants and establishing a reputation as a cradle of managers and one of the great teams of all time, they hadn't made much money.

Ebbets and Von der Horst decided they could put Baltimore's players—Wee Willie Keeler, Joe Kelley and Dan McGann for example—with Brooklyn's population of fans and come up with a winner on and off the field.

The two camps struck a deal to split ownership of both franchises. Baltimore manager Ned Hanlon would come to Brooklyn as manager and part-owner. Ebbets would remain as team president. Von der Horst and Hanlon would own fifty percent, as would Abell and Ebbets. Ebbets' share was variously reported as nine percent and ten percent. Hanlon's was ten percent.

The deal was a success in Brooklyn. The team won the 1899 National League race and drew 269,641 fans, 120 percent more than a year before. They won again in 1900, although attendance slumped to about 183,000.

But soon Brooklyn lost stars such as Keeler and "Iron Man" Joe McGinnity to the American League, which had proclaimed itself a major league in 1901 and begun raids on the senior circuit. Attendance fell. Ebbets' partners were skittish.

Von der Horst had become unhappy with Hanlon for reasons that remain obscure. His confidante on the team was now Ebbets. Early in 1905, Ebbets was able to persuade an ailing Von der Horst to sell him virtually all of his shares. Ebbets' newest financial angel was a Brooklyn furniture manufacturer named Henry W. Medicus. Medicus was an old friend of Ebbets. The two had been extremely active in Brooklyn bowling circles for years. Medicus was elected an officer of the team and kept some shares in his name, but he was willing to remain even further in the background than Von der Horst.[18] This gave Ebbets effective control of the team, although his personal holdings were well less than fifty percent.

By the end of the year, Von der Horst had died and Hanlon had signed to manage the Cincinnati Reds. It wasn't until November, 1907 that Ebbets got rid of Hanlon completely. At that time, he and Medicus bought out Abell, Hanlon and the tiny holding of Von der Horst's estate. Ebbets announced he controlled seventy percent of the team, including ten percent owned by Charles Ebbets Jr., while Medicus had the rest. Medicus again provided most of the cash, although the shares were in Ebbets' name.[19]

The team entered a period of relative prosperity. Attendance was steady (averaging about 238,000 over the decade of the 1900s) even if the team wasn't performing very well. In 1909, at a post-season banquet, the long-winded Ebbets reviewed the history of baseball and concluded the sport was still in its infancy. The audience dissolved in laughter and Ebbets was nearly heckled off the stage. But he believed what he said, and was emboldened to try his most enduring venture.

A new ballpark—As a business, baseball had stabilized. The erratic franchises, the tottery leagues and the incomplete schedules of the nineteenth century had disappeared. When the prosperity which followed the death of the Players' League and American Association in the early 1890s ended, the League cut back to eight from twelve teams. Rather than fighting tooth and nail, as it had with earlier rivals, the National League struck a deal with Ban Johnson's new American League after only two seasons.

With the end of salary wars, and with the reserve clause firmly in place, the teams' biggest cost was under control. Players pretty much had to take whatever salary was offered.

Franchise values had increased, with the average team worth perhaps $150,000. Between 1901 and 1907, major league attendance increased from three million to six million, and then went over seven million in 1908. For the years from 1909 to 1913, the average team had annual revenue of over $250,000.[20]

The general prosperity led major league owners to deal with one of their most persistent problems—the quality of their facilities. Wooden grandstands were cheap to erect, but they crumbled, collapsed and burned.

In 1909, the Philadelphia Athletics opened Shibe Park, the first of the concrete and steel stadiums. In the next few years, it was followed by similar structures around both leagues. Washington Park was a wooden firetrap in an often smoky industrial area near the malodorous Gowanus Canal. Ebbets had added so many seats that he'd severely restricted foul territory. Its main advantage was its central location, but Brooklyn's center was moving south and east. For several years beginning in 1908, Ebbets painstakingly put together pieces of land in a neighborhood then called Pigtown. The property was occupied by garbage dumps and squatters. It was owned by a collection of people, from whom Ebbets had to hide his intentions for fear of driving up the prices. He formed a corporate cover and named it by opening the dictionary and randomly poking the word "pylon." Pylon Construction Company's last purchase involved chasing a property owner from California to Berlin to Paris only to run him to earth in the more prosaic Montclair, New Jersey. The last deed was recorded Dec. 29, 1911.[21]

His site, as Ebbets noted excitedly in a letter to August Herrmann, chairman of the National Commission, the three-man body which oversaw baseball before the commissioner system, was served by nine mass transit lines. "Between 3,000,000 and 4,000,000 people can reach the new site by surface, subway or elevated in thirty to forty-five minutes." It was within easy reach of the older neighborhoods, but poised to be in the middle of the borough's future expansion.[22]

In January 1912, Ebbets announced he had put together the parcel and intended the Dodgers to have a concrete and steel ballpark on the site. Asked what he would call it, Ebbets said he didn't know, but the reporters began calling it Ebbets Field.

Ebbets began construction in March 1912. His public cost estimate was $750,000 including land. But, in his letter to Herrmann, he gave a construction budget of about $325,000 plus almost $200,000 for the land, $100,000 of which had already been paid. He estimated the remaining $425,000 would be raised from a bond sale of $275,000, a bank loan for $100,000 that he would secure personally, and the team's $50,000 profit from 1912. He was probably closer with the public estimate.

The 18,000-seat stadium was supposed to be finished by June, or maybe August. It wasn't. Excuses were given about undelivered materials and labor agitation.[23] Apparently, though, the real trouble was money. In late August, Ebbets announced he had bought out Medicus and taken new partners. They were two politically well-connected brothers, Ed and Steve McKeever, who were in the construction business. Ebbets wouldn't say how much the brothers' stake was, but subsequent events were to prove they each had received twenty-five percent of the team for their investments.

The McKeevers—The brothers McKeever had a textbook career on how the nineteenth-century Irish got ahead. Steve was born in 1852 and Ed in 1859, both in Brooklyn. Both received minimal educations, Steve's being interrupted when he ran away in an unsuccessful attempt to join the Union Army as a drummer boy. He went to work as a horse boy for a trolley line down near the Fulton Street Ferry and was eventually apprenticed to a plumber. Ed also left school at 14, first working for a brass wholesaler and then joining with Michael J. Daly to form the Hudson River Broken Stone Company.[24]

Within a few years, the brothers combined their expertise in plumbing and stone work to form the E.J. & S.W. McKeever Contracting Company. They had also learned well from Daly, who got government contracts through his excellent political contacts. When Steve McKeever married in 1892, one of his ushers was Hugh McLaughlin, boss of the Brooklyn Democratic party. One of the company's first contracts was for plumbing work on the Brooklyn Bridge. The McKeevers built their company constructing sewers and water mains, and paving streets. And, they had a lucrative city contract to take Brooklyn's garbage out to sea and dump it. When the McKeevers' identities were revealed, sportswriters outdid each other suggesting which of the Dodgers should be given one-way rides on the brothers' fleet of scows.[25]

How much the brothers paid for their shares isn't clear. Most of the contemporary sources refer to a figure of $100,000, but *The Sporting News* obituary of Steve McKeever says it was $250,000 and Robert Creamer's biography of Casey Stengel lists it as $500,000.[26] Part of this investment may not have been in cash, as the McKeevers evidently turned some of their expertise to finishing the new stadium on time and at less cost.

Uncle Robbie—Attendance rose forty-three percent to 347,000. With more income and the McKeevers' bankroll behind him, Ebbets brought Wilbert Robinson in as manager and began to invest in ballplayers. Casey Stengel had arrived during the last year in Washington Park, joining Zack Wheat. In the next couple of years, Ebbets, Robinson and scout Larry Sutton added Jeff Pfeffer, Larry Cheney, Sherry Smith and Rube Marquard, the nucleus of the team that would win the 1916 pennant.

The pennant-winning season ushered in a prosperous era, which would leave Charles Ebbets with an estate worth over $1 million. The improvement started with the quality of the team. A second pennant was added in 1920 and an unexpectedly fine team in 1924 led to a tight pennant race and another attendance record. It was helped by the new stadium, which was expanded to 22,000 seats for the 1917 season.

The second boost was the collapse of the Federal League after the 1915 season. The Federal League lasted two years and had little success either on or off the field. Ebbets had to compete with a Federal League franchise in Brooklyn, but did so successfully at the gate. He even managed a $30,000 profit in 1914, while the Brooklyn Federals lost $800,000 in 1915.[27] He also had to compete with the Feds on salaries. In 1916, many of those salaries persisted because of the multiyear contracts that had been used to tie up the better players. After that year, however, despite the team's pennant, his own new franchise attendance record, and the ticket prices he'd raised during the 1916 season, Ebbets embarked on wholesale salary cutting for 1917.

The third factor that helped Ebbets was the final victory of Sunday baseball, in 1919. In a day when many working people still labored six days a week, the ability to stage a game on their day off was a tremendous shot in the arm for attendance.

The fourth factor was sheer population growth. By 1920, Brooklyn's population hit two million, an increase of twenty-three percent for the decade. By 1930, Brooklyn had passed Manhattan as the city's most populous borough and Flatbush was in the center of the growth.

Ebbets died near the peak of his success as an owner. He fell ill early in 1925 and died of heart failure in April in the suite at the Waldorf-Astoria Hotel which he now could afford. His funeral was held on a raw day and when the cortege got to Greenwood Cemetery, it was discovered the grave had been dug too small for the casket. The funeral party, including Ed McKeever, stood in the rain for an hour while gravediggers widened the muddy hole. McKeever caught a cold, which turned into pneumonia and killed him only eleven days later.

The team's ownership was thrown into turmoil and a pattern was set which was to last for thirteen years. Management was weak and when the Depression hit, the losses put the team effectively in control of its lenders.

Ebbets had had a somewhat involved family life and left multiple heirs. His estate was divided into 15ths. Joseph Gilleaudeau, husband of Ebbets' daughter, Genevieve, served on the board, but with a fragmented family behind him, he could offer little direction.[28]

Ed McKeever's heirs were also divided. His estate was broken into 18ths, as he provided for several nieces and other relatives. Steve McKeever took up a more active role, but his baseball experience was limited. He was soon at loggerheads with Wilbert Robinson, who had been named the team's president with the support of the Ebbets family. The two men literally snarled epithets such as "rat" at each other across their small offices above the rotunda at Ebbets Field.[29]

More bad times—It was just the beginning of a precipitous decline in the franchise. In a review of the team's status soon after the deaths, the *New York Times* described the Dodgers as "one of the soundest organizations financially in professional baseball." It was a team that sparked buyer interest. Former Yankees owner Tillinghast Huston was reported interested, as was former Boston Braves owner James Gaffney. A local developer and song and dance man George M. Cohan were also mentioned. In 1928, there was a brief stir when it was reported mayor Jimmy Walker, with the financial backing of publisher Paul Block, would make a bid. A month later, the rumored bidder was former Pittsburgh Pirates great Honus Wagner. But the buying interest soon drifted away as the management fell behind on the mortgage and turned the team into the joke of the league. Not always the worst team, mind you, but definitely a joke.[30]

Eventually, the National League stepped in, naming a president to arbitrate between the two factions. Robinson was eased out, first as president and then as manager. But the unity among management had come too late. When John Quinn, an experienced baseball executive, was brought in to run the team, he was struck by the utter listlessness of the front office.[31] Managers were fired in the desperate hope of sparking fan interest because the players weren't going to get any better. Thus, with a team losing money, the club's directors were paying two managers in both 1934 (Max Carey and Casey Stengel) and 1937 (Stengel and Burleigh Grimes).

Mismanagement was widespread. After a big season in 1930, the directors decided to expand the stadium by replacing the wooden bleachers behind left field with concrete stands. They borrowed $600,000 from the bank. When the job was completed, the directors found to their horror that there weren't any additional seats. The case wound up in court. And the consequent appearance of anxious bankers on the club's board did little good. One protested the purchase of a player for a Dodger farm team because, he said, the team didn't need any farmers.

And then there was the Depression. Team attendance peaked in 1930, when they drew just over a million fans for the first time. The number of paying fans had dropped to 434,188 by 1934 and had stayed at that level. The team even began to look like the most disadvantaged of its fans. During spring training in the mid-'30s, the wonderfully named clubhouse man Babe Hamberger would set up a sewing machine outside the dressing room to fix rips in the already patched team uniforms.[33]

Even with their fans, who were more vociferous than numerous, the Dodgers had fallen on exceedingly hard times by the end of the 1937 season. They had last made a profit in 1930. Phone service had been cut off because the bills weren't being paid. The team's office was crowded with process servers seeking payment. Ebbets Field was a mass of broken seats, begging for a paint job. Charles Ebbets' pride, the beautiful rotunda, was covered with mildew. The team's officials had begun to seek the solace of banks, owing over half a million dollars. Its office address became 215 Montague St., in the Brooklyn Trust Co. building.

The Brooklyn Trust Co. was the team's bank, and by late 1937, the Dodgers owed it $700,000, $470,000 of that on a refinanced mortgage for Ebbets Field. It had lost $129,140 in 1937.[34]

Larry MacPhail—The board remained divided, with the Ebbets and McKeever blocks unable to reach agreement. George V. McLaughlin, the Brooklyn Trust Co.'s president, was anxious to be repaid. He cut off any future advances to the team unless the board found a strong executive. Thrashing around for a solution, Jim Mulvey, who was married to Steve McKeever's daughter, Dearie, approached St. Louis Cardinals' vice president Branch Rickey with an offer to take over the team. Rickey said no, but suggested he might have someone who wanted the job, Leland Stanford "Larry" MacPhail.

When he came to Brooklyn, the 47-year-old MacPhail carried a large and speckled reputation. Born in Michigan, MacPhail had gotten his law degree and made a success of retailing in Nashville. During World War I, he had joined a Tennessee regiment. He was nicked by shrapnel and caught a whiff of poison gas, but the war story he loved to tell happened after the cease fire. MacPhail joined a scheme to kidnap the German Kaiser, who was in retirement in Holland after the war. The hare-brained escapade was unsuccessful, although MacPhail forever after kept a bronze ashtray embossed with W I (Wilhelm Imperator) on his desk.

MacPhail was a florid man in hair, complexion, dress and manner. He was verbally aggressive, but those who talked back found there were no penalties involved. One secretary got her job, and kept it for years, after a confrontation with MacPhail in her first hours.

MacPhail took the first steps toward creating the solid franchise the Dodgers are today. Some of those changes were cosmetic, but others were fundamental.

The cosmetics began with $200,000 McLaughlin had agreed to provide before MacPhail would take the job. Ebbets Field was painted. Its many broken seats were repaired. The infamous corps of usher–thugs was weeded out and re-trained. One afternoon in MacPhail's first year, the unemployed Babe Ruth walked into the ballpark. MacPhail noticed that far more people watched Ruth in the stands than the hapless Dodgers on the field. The next day, Ruth was hired as a coach.

MacPhail had his eye on a new manager, too, a loud-mouthed, light-hitting, clotheshorse who was playing shortstop for the team. Leo Durocher was one of MacPhail's non-cosmetic moves. Another was using an additional $50,000 from McLaughlin to buy first baseman Dolph Camilli from the even more hapless Phillies.

MacPhail scheduled Brooklyn's first night game, and was rewarded when the fates tossed up Cincinnati lefthander Johnny Vander Meer as the opposing pitcher. Vander Meer's last outing had been a no-hitter, and under the lights that night, he became the only pitcher ever to throw consecutive no-hitters. In 1939, with Durocher as manager, the team moved into a competitive third-place finish and the fans started to come back.

MacPhail also broke the gentlemen's agreement among New York teams not to broadcast their games on radio. He imported Red Barber from Cincinnati and locked up a powerful station and a strong sponsor before the Yankees or the Giants moved. It took Brooklyn fans a while to get used to Barber's Southernisms such as the catbird seat and the rhubarb patch, but once they did, he became a valuable tool for building interest in the improving product on the field.

O'Malley arrives—Within four years, MacPhail had won a pennant, lured over a million people to Ebbets Field for the first time and, at McLaughlin's suggestion, hired on a young little-known Brooklyn lawyer named Walter Francis O'Malley.

McLaughlin's suggestion carried more the force of an order, for he wasn't totally happy about the Dodgers' financial direction. MacPhail was a wonderful promoter, a whirlwind dealmaker, a genius for creating interest. MacPhail was a disaster as an administrator. He was also skirting the bounds of corporate ethics. When he needed a little money for the race track, he'd dip into the petty cash drawer.[35] Even without MacPhail's venial sins, the team's administration was a mess. O'Malley found the team was grossing somewhere between $2.5 million and $4 million, but couldn't tell where in between. One $100-a-week official fired by O'Malley quickly bought a large motel in Florida and said he'd saved the money up from his salary.[36]

After a year of O'Malley's administration, as McLaughlin eased MacPhail out the door and into the Army, the short-term loans had been repaid and the mortgage reduced to $350,000. There was a cash balance of $100,000.

Rickey—MacPhail was succeeded by the man who inserted the rest of the puzzle pieces. Branch Rickey had put together the majors' first farm system while he was with the St. Louis Cardinals. Brooklyn, strapped for cash, had only one farm team when MacPhail took over. MacPhail had added several teams, but Rickey proceeded to stock them.

In 1942, Branch Rickey made the simple calculation that World War II would end some day. Other teams, fearing the effects of the war, were cutting back on scouting and signing prospects on the theory they would soon be swept into the armed forces. Rickey operated on the theory they would eventually get out, and he signed as many talented people as he could find. When the war ended, the Dodger camps and farm teams bulged with prospects. They produced seven pennants in the next 14 campaigns, plus three more teams which lost either in playoffs or on the last day of the season.

Rickey also turned to another source of talent—black ballplayers. With the signings of Jackie Robinson, Roy Campanella and Don Newcombe in the years immediately after the war, he added immeasurably to the Dodgers' talent pool.

The success led to the first change in ownership in many years. When Steve McKeever had died in 1938, his twenty-five percent interest had passed to his daughter, Dearie, usually represented by her husband, airline executive James A. Mulvey. It had meant little to the control of the team, which was then still effectively in the hands of the Brooklyn Trust Co.

By 1944, the situation had changed. The eradication of the team's debt had made the Ebbets and Ed McKeever shares, which had been held as collateral by Brooklyn Trust, much more salable. The prosperity and prospects of the team had created interested buyers.

In November, 1944, the first sale was announced. Rickey, O'Malley and a Brooklyn insurance man named Andrew J. Schmitz bought the twenty-five percent of the team owned by Ed McKeever's heirs for a reported $250,000. Less than a year later, in August, 1945, Rickey, O'Malley and John L. Smith, president of Pfizer Chemical Corp., bought the Ebbets family's fifty percent. Smith, it turned out, had been a silent partner in the first purchase

and Schmitz faded from the scene.[37]

Each of the three partners owned twenty-five percent, with Dearie and James Mulvey controlling the remainder.

With personalities as strong as Rickey's and O'Malley's, it was inevitable there wouldn't be room enough for both. James Mulvey had been very instrumental in recruiting Rickey to join the Dodgers, so he was presumably firmly in the Rickey camp.

Smith would inevitably be the swing man, for with his votes, O'Malley could effectively block any further extension of Rickey's contract as president and general manager. Smith had made his business reputation as the man who had figured out how to mass produce penicillin during World War II. At first, he seemed inclined to Rickey. The men were co-religionists and shared many other interests. O'Malley eventually won Smith and his wife over. Partially, it was the famous O'Malley charm. But it was also a series of business decisions that Rickey and O'Malley fought over, and Smith's judgment of whose business acumen was better came to be crucial.[38]

The issues ran from the trivial to the pivotal. O'Malley, for example, fought a move to give every Dodger player and coach a Studebaker after losing to the Cardinals in a playoff in 1946.

O'Malley strongly opposed Rickey's decision to invest in an old airfield just outside Vero Beach, Florida and turn it into a spring training camp. He expressed himself unhappy over the money Rickey was spending on the farm system. He objected to Rickey's habit of selling the surplus of the farm system (and pocketing a percentage Rickey's contract gave him).

On other issues, O'Malley clearly seemed to be more thoughtful. He unsuccessfully opposed Rickey's decision to invest in a professional football team in the All-America Conference which was also called the Brooklyn Dodgers. From that conference, the Cleveland Browns and San Francisco 49ers went on to the National Football League. The football Dodgers went on to run up a $750,000 loss, and Rickey looked no better for such schemes as signing former St. Louis Cardinal great Pepper Martin as a place kicker. He saved Rickey from a libel suit after the extremely conservative Rickey described a couple of players who jumped to the Mexican League and their lawyer as having "avowed Communistic tendencies."

On yet others, it was simply a clash of generations and backgrounds. He and Rickey fought over whether the club should let a brewery sponsor Dodger games. O'Malley and the brewery won. Rickey turned down $150,000 for the Dodgers' television rights in 1949, drawing the ire of O'Malley. Rickey argued that television would hurt attendance and destroy the minor leagues. O'Malley saw it as another source of revenue.

With Smith's growing regard and failing health, it was becoming clear to Rickey that O'Malley was going to be able to impose his will on the team, for Mrs. Smith showed support for O'Malley after her husband died in

1950. Should Mrs. Smith sell, her shares would have to be offered first to both Rickey and O'Malley, and only O'Malley had the money to buy them.

Making use of the same agreement, Rickey worked out his own plan, for Walter O'Malley wasn't the only shrewd operator at 215 Montague Street. Rickey lined up support from John Galbreath, the Pirates' owner who'd been trying to recruit him as general manager. He got Galbreath to find him a bidder for his share of the team. Real estate tycoon William Zeckendorf offered $1,050,000 for Rickey's quarter interest in the team. O'Malley whined, fumed and paid. Rickey got $1 million, Zeckendorf got a $50,000 broker's fee, and O'Malley got control of the Dodgers.

His outright ownership was fifty percent of the shares, but he also had an option on one percent owned by Mrs. Smith. He had more absolute control over the franchise than any executive in its history. Seven years later, he exercised that control by moving the team from Brooklyn to Los Angeles, making major league baseball a truly national sport.

Mrs. Smith remained on the team's board until the early 1960s. Dearie Mulvey's heirs sold out in January, 1975. Only then, for the first time in the history of the team, did one man own the franchise outright.

But it was a short-lived unity. In August, 1979, Walter O'Malley died. His shares were divided among his son Peter, who runs the team, and his daughter, Teresa O'Malley Seidler. Teresa and her husband, stockbroker Roland Seidler, both sit on the team's board.

Notes

[2] New York *Clipper*, March 4, 1899, p. 11 for the $12,000 figure. Contemporary accounts referred to $14,000 (New York Clipper, March 10, 1883, p. 818).

[3] There are some discrepancies among the sources about when Abell joined the ownership group. *The New York Times* and *Sporting Life* obituaries of Charles Byrne assert that Abell (in both) and Doyle (in *Sporting Life*) didn't join the partnership until it was in the American Association. But the New York *Clipper* of March 17, 1883, page 840, notes the incorporation of the team and Abell's and Doyle's names lead the list. Abell's name is occasionally spelled Abel.

[4] *The Sporting Life*, October 19, 1884, p. 4.

[5] *The Sporting Life*, April 9, 1884, p. 4, April 15, 1885, p. 7.

[6] The *New York Clipper*, March 4, 1899, p. 11, says Taylor left the team's ownership between the 1885 and 1886 seasons, but no other sources confirm this.

[7] *The Sporting Life*, Jan. 8, 1898, p. 5.

[9] *The Sporting Life*, Jan. 8, 1898, p. 5.

[10] *The Sporting News*, Jan. 23, 1892, p. 5.

[11] Graham, *Brooklyn Dodgers*, p. 7, mentions Chauncey's sale of some shares to Ebbets, but I have found no other source for this.

[12] *The Sporting Life*, Jan. 8, 1898, p. 5.

[13] Ebbets, "History of Baseball in Brooklyn," *Brooklyn Eagle*, Feb. 21, 1913.

[14] Ibid, March 1, 1913.

[16] Lieb, Fred, *Baseball As I Have Known It*. New York: Coward, McCann & Geoghegan, Inc., 1977, p. 268.

[17] Allen, *The Giants and the Dodgers*, pp. 127-8.

[18] Seymour, v. 2, p. 128.

[19] Contemporary sources varied greatly in their estimates of how big a share was owned by the Players' League group, and thus the franchise value implied for it. The reports varied from 22.5 percent (*New York Times*, Jan. 21, 1912, pt. 4, p. 3, col. 1) to 40 percent (*The Sporting News*, Jan. 8, 1898, p. 4). However, in the same issue of the next page, *The Sporting News* gave a breakdown of team ownership which said the Players League group owned about 35 percent.

[20] *New York Times*, Jan. 31, 1898, p. 4, col. 7.

[21] *The Sporting News*, March 25, 1905, p. 1.

[22] *The Sporting News*, Nov. 7, 1907, p. 5; *The Sporting Life*, Nov. 9, 1907, p. 2.

[23] The estimate of franchise values appeared in the *New York Times* Dec. 30, 1906, p. 12, col. 3; the average team revenue figure is calculated from *Organized Baseball, Hearings before the Subcommittee on Study of Monopoly Power of the Committee on the Judiciary, House of Representatives*, 1952, p. 1616.

[25] Graham, *Brooklyn Dodgers*, p. 24. The best discussion of the construction of Ebbets Field is an unpublished paper by Matthew Kachur, "Brooklyn, Baseball, and Ebbets Field."

[26] Letter, Ebbets to Herrmann, May 12, 1912, contained in the Herrmann papers at the National Baseball Hall of Fame and Museum in Cooperstown, N.Y.

[27] *The Sporting Life*, Aug. 17, 1912, p. 7. *The Sporting Life*, Aug. 24, 1912, p. 3.

[28] Background on the McKeevers is mostly drawn from obituaries. Edward's, *New York Times*, April 30, 1925, p. 1, col. 5. Steve's, *New York Times*, March 7, 1938, p. 17, col. 1 and *The Sporting News*, March 10, 1938, p. 7.

[29] *New York Times*, Sept. 6, 1892, p. 5, col. 5. The garbage scow anecdote was in Fred Lieb's column in *The Sporting News*, November 16, 1944, p. 8.

[30] *The Sporting News*, March 10, 1938, p. 7. Robert Creamer's figure appears in *Stengel*, New York: Simon and Schuster, 1984, p. 59.

[31] The 1914 Dodger profit figure: Allen, *Giants and Dodgers*, p. 97. The Brooklyn Federals loss is in Hailey, Gary, "Anatomy of a Murder: The Federal League and the Courts." *The National Pastime*, Society for American Baseball Research, Spring 1985, p. 66.

[33] McKeever's will is described in the *New York Times*, May 9, 1925, p. 3, col. 2, and in *The Sporting News*, May 14, 1925, p. 2. The "rat" quote is in Graham, *The Brooklyn Dodgers*, p. 116.

[34] *New York Times*, May 1, 1925, p. 21, col. 5; Jan. 11, 1928, p. 35, col 2; Feb. 25, 1928, p. 13, col. 1.

[35] Tommy Holmes, *The Dodgers*. New York: Macmillan, 1975, p. 26.

[36] Creamer, *Stengel*, p. 184.

[37] The $600,000 figure is in Holmes, Tommy, *Dodger Daze and Knight*, p. 80. The suit was reported in *The Sporting News*, Dec. 24, 1931, p. 17. The farmers story is in Tom Meany and Bill McCullough's "Once a Dodger", in Ed Fitzgerald, ed. *The Story of the Brooklyn Dodgers*, New York: Bantam Books, 1949, p. 39.

[38] Meany, Tom, *The Magnificent Yankees*, New York: Grosset & Dunlap, 1957, p. 30.

[39] Mann, Arthur, "The Larry MacPhail Story, Part One." *Sport*, Vol. 21., No. 4 (April 1956), 76.

[40] Parrott, Harold, *The Lords of Baseball*, New York: Praeger Publishers, 1976.

[41] Kahn, Roger, *Good Enough to Dream*, New York: Doubleday, 1985, p. 56.

[42] *The Sporting News*, Nov. 9, 1944, p. 1, February 1, 1945, p. 9, August 16, 1945, p. 4.

[43] Polner, Murray, *Branch Rickey: A Biography*, New York: Atheneum, 1982, pp. 215-225.

Young and a Giant

Bill Chambers

Ⅰt was late August 1970, the last weekend before my friend Bob and I went back to college for our senior year. Ten o'clock Saturday morning, the time we'd agreed upon. Larry Doyle, eighty-four years old, met us at the door of his modest house in Saranac Lake, New York.

"Call me Larry, all my friends do." His smile was warm, his enthusiasm infectious. We liked him immediately.

I had become a Larry Doyle fan in a roundabout way. I had been a rabid follower of the New York Giants, one of the tens of thousands who felt abandoned when the team moved to the West Coast in 1958. Sometime after that at a flea market I picked up a copy of *The Real McGraw* and was particularly intrigued by Laughing Larry Doyle, his pepperpot second baseman from 1907 through 1920. "It's great to be young and a Giant," he once said. That one line emphasized his great distance from contemporary ballplayers and endeared him to me forever. Larry Doyle became the object of my revitalized baseball affections, and my window to baseball history.

Bob and I wrote requesting an interview. Doyle graciously agreed. All was right with the world. (It's great to be young and a Larry Doyle fan.)

We found him more than willing to talk baseball history. He loved to hit in old Redland—later Crosley—Field. Dutch Ruether was the toughest pitcher he faced. Eight thousand was his highest salary, and he seemed proud that that was the same year Christy Mathewson made eleven thousand. He tried Ty Cobb's peculiar split-grip batting style but was never comfortable

This article is adapted from Bill Chambers' presentation, "Larry Doyle's Field of Dreams," which won the John W. Cox award at SABR's 1992 National Convention .

Smile! Laughing Larry stretches for the camera.

with it. He was never the same, he confessed, after a broken leg forced him to miss most of the 1917 season. He showed us his batting stance, his scrapbooks and many picture albums. Signing a photo of himself from his playing days, he seemed for one moment a trifle sad and misty-eyed.

Naturally we asked him about the 1908 pennant race and the famous Merkle incident. I knew that Doyle had been Fred Merkle's roommate at the time, that they regularly played pool together after games and were close friends. We were surprised, then, when he said, "Bonehead play. Just a stupid play." That made Doyle, to my knowledge, the only Giant who ever spoke critically of Merkle's play.

We had intended to take him to lunch, but he would not hear of it. Instead he treated us to a ballpark meal of hot dogs and Coca-Colas. When our stay ended, he invited us back for the next day.

We returned with a surprise—a board game in which old World Series games could be replayed. We decided on the 1911 Series. Of course we would manage the Philadelphia A's and Doyle would direct his own Giants.

In the ninth inning his Giants were losing 3-2. Two out, two on, and the last hope was—Larry Doyle himself. The real-life Doyle looked at us and said, "Well, this is it. I'd better come through." He spun the game's wheel, and I

Fred Merkle: "Just a stupid play."

said a little prayer, which was answered. The table-top Doyle doubled home the tying run.

The game went into extra innings. In the twelfth, Doyle walked and promptly ordered himself sacrificed to second. He then lifted one of his regulars, Red Murray, for a pinch hitter, Beals Becker. We asked him why, and without hesitation he replied that Becker had always hit A's pitcher Cy Morgan like he owned him. Sure enough, Becker singled home Doyle with the winning run. Normally such a game lasts about an hour, but ours had taken nearly three. Almost every situation and every play had reminded him of a story.

Afterward we talked more baseball until time grew short. We had almost 400 miles of driving ahead, and our host, fresh from victory, had had a long day himself. Still, leaving saddened me. Larry Doyle was everything I had hoped he would be, larger than life in every way. I marveled at how much he still knew, how much he truly loved the game.

When I heard the news of his death early in 1974, I cried. I recalled his kindness, his happiness, the way he shared his memories and his love of baseball. I cherish the memory of the time when we helped make Larry Doyle "young and a New York Giant" again.

Denny Lyons' 52-Game Hitting Streak

David Q. Voigt

In celebrating the golden anniversary of Joe DiMaggio's enduring 56-game hitting streak, pundits of 1991 vied with one another for the pithiest paeans. The general refrain amongst this reverential din touted the streak as the all-time individual batting achievement and the most admired record in sports history.

The hyperbolics drowned out most dissenters, but not Gene Case. Writing in *The Nation* that fall, iconoclast Case belittled the streak as a product of statistical hype, an early spurting of the great gusher of statistics that now pollutes baseball coverage. And in a gallant effort to de-mythologize the streak, Case cited seven 20th century hitters who exceeded DiMaggio's .408 batting over the course of 56 games. Heading the pack was Rogers Hornsby, who hit .480 during 56 games in 1922, and George Brett, who batted .465 over a similar route in 1980. Of course, not one of Case's magnificent seven managed to hit safely in 56 consecutive games.

But Case was on target in fingering consecutive game hitting streaks as a rather recent concoction by statistical zealots. In fact, when DiMaggio launched his streak in May, 1941, not only was such a feat barely recognized as a batting prowess, but the goal was unclear. Thus when New York writers took to touting the streak, they first fixed on George Sisler's 1922 skein of 41 straight games and belatedly revised the goal upon discovering Willie Keeler's 1897 string of 44 consecutive games. Indeed, Keeler hit safely in his first 44 games (with recent re-

search suggesting 45) and went on to bat .432 during that 132-game National League campaign. In 1941, the discovery of Keeler's achievement heaped added pressure on DiMaggio, who not only met the challenge, but surpassed the mark by a dozen games.

Luckily, DiMaggio was spared the mental agony of having to surpass an even longer hitting streak, one that escaped the scrutiny of 1941 statisticians and still eludes most figure filberts. It was the string of 52 consecutive games compiled by Dennis Patrick Aloysius Lyons of the American Association Philadelphia Athletics during the summer of 1887. For this revelation, credit goes to researcher Bill Gottlieb of the National Baseball Library. Had Lyons' streak been known in 1941, one can only speculate how DiMaggio would have reacted to the added pressure.

At least in 1941, Lyons' record would have been recognized as official. The wrong-headed "revision" of the 1887 records by Special Records Committee of 1968 had not come to pass. Indeed, the current revelation of Lyons' streak fuels the controversy over the quixotic 1968 records revisions, and poses a reminder to baseball historians of the uncertainties that still lurk in the uncharted shoals of 120 years of major league baseball records.

The "radical" rule changes of 1887—Lyons' formidable record was made possible by sweeping changes in the major league playing and scoring rules that were adopted for the 1887 season. Such changes were typical of the game's adolescent years, as rule makers struggled to strike a balance between hitting and pitching performances. During the early 1880s, drastic rule changes were annual occurrences. Although hitters rejoiced when

David Q. Voigt is a professor at Albright College and is currently working on a book, The League That Failed, *that deals with the "big league" of the 1890s.*

the pitching distance was extended to fifty feet in 1881, pitchers regained dominance when overhand pitching was officially permitted in 1884. As a result, seasonal strikeouts soared and batting averages plummeted over the next three seasons. This was the situation in 1886, when pitchers benefited from a seven-ball count before a batter could take his base, and also intimidated batters by moving deceptively within the confines of their 4-ft. by 7-ft. pitching boxes. As for the over-matched hitters, their only advantage was the continuance of the long-established rule that allowed them to choose a high or a low strike zone.

To redress the pitching imbalance for the 1887 season, the two major leagues established the first Joint Committee on Rules, staffed it with officials and player representatives from each circuit, and charged the group with the task of overhauling the playing rules. In November, 1886, the committee met for a week of "careful thought and study" and unanimously agreed on a list of "radical" changes aimed mainly at jump-starting sagging offenses. To this end, the base-on-ball count was lowered to five balls, the strike count was increased to four, a batter hit by a pitch could take his base, and flat-sided bats were allowed. Moreover, pitchers were required to face a batter with one foot on the back line of the box before delivering a pitch.

As one might surmise, no active pitcher served on the committee, but pitchers at least were given a single strike zone extending from a batter's shoulder to his knee. A rule imposing a called strike for deliberate foul balls was another sop thrown to pitchers who faced the prospect of a tough season in 1887.

Although the new rules guaranteed a healthy hitting environment, it was the scoring change that credited bases on balls as hits that rocketed 1887 batting averages to record heights. In defending this radical innovation, the committee argued that it was "rewarding the careful waiter on balls" and that "a base on balls is as good as a base hit and will now be exactly the same."

After receiving the unanimous report from the committee, the two major leagues speedily voted to accept all of the proposals. By the end of December, 1886 the new rules, including the scoring of a hit for a walk, were duly certified as official practice for organized baseball's upcoming 1887 season. Thus, the official status of the 1887 records is a stubborn historical fact, one that baseball historians are pledged to accept. The attempted revision of the 1887 batting records by the 1968 records committee constitutes an act of real violence to the integrity of official records.

While no argument can justify the 1968 committee's crime, some revisionists now compound the offense by attempting to spin a myth of universal opposition to the base-on-balls-equals-a-hit rule in its 1887 setting. This myth smacks of gnosticism and is not borne out by contemporary reportage. Indeed, at the time the rules were adopted, John Ward, who served on the Joint Committee, exulted that the changes were endorsed by leading baseball figures, including Ned Hanlon, Henry Chadwick, and George and Harry Wright, and he urged that the new rules be given a fair trial.

Nor was there much opposition to the rules during the 1887 season. Indeed, *The Sporting Life* noted only a single dissenting voice, that of Cincinnati third baseman "Hick" Carpenter, who attacked the controversial scoring rule, saying, "I don't fancy...crediting a man with a base hit every time he gets his base on balls. It isn't ball playing...to give a batter as much credit for standing like a stick as...the man who smashes the ball on the nose for a clean hit."

As for organized opposition to the scoring rule, the only hint came when *The Sporting Life* scolded Boston writers for conspiring against the rule by denying batters a hit for a walk. The journal denounced the conspiracy in these withering words: "There is just as much sense in the Boston scribes flocking by themselves and scoring after their own peculiar ideas as there would...a lawyer trying to apply his own ideas to a case because the authorities didn't suit him." The article assured fans that "all newspapers in the country except those in Boston" accepted the new scoring rule. And it was this rule that abetted Denny Lyons' splendid performance of 1887.

Lyons' Unsung Hitting Streak—In the spring of 1887 Denny Lyons was a 21-year-old third baseman hoping to play his first full season in the major leagues. Behind him were two years of minor league seasoning during which he showed promise enough to be summoned briefly by major league teams. In 1885 he had played a few games with the NL Providence team, and in 1886 he'd played some thirty games with the AA Philadelphia Athletics. With the A's, Lyons was good enough to be ticketed as the team's starter at third in 1887.

That March, Lyons, a 5'–7" right-handed batter and thrower, joined the A's for spring training. At a rented skating rink in Philadelphia, Athletic captain Harry Stovey put his men on a daily regimen of batting, throwing, and fielding practice that was augmented by handball and racquet play.

As a charter member of the six-year-old American Association, the A's had fallen on losing ways after winning the 1883 pennant. In 1887, the team's immediate goal was to better the sixth-place finish of 1886, which had dumped them 28 games behind the reigning world champion St. Louis Browns. To this end, owner Bill Sharsig hired Frank Bancroft, who had piloted the 1884 NL Providence team to a world title. Manager Bancroft's grim task was to mold a winner from a young team whose ranks included two 20-year-old rookie pitchers and two 21-year-old infielders, including Lyons.

Although Lyons had shown some promise as a hitter, his limited experience gave no hint of an imminent erup-

Denny Lyons showing off other skills, the year after his streak.

tion. On the contrary, after batting .230 and .316 in the Southern League, he had hit only .226 in 32 games with the 1886 A's. That inauspicious debut preyed on the mind of the local reporter who watched Lyons in spring training and cautiously noted that, although he had shed 15 pounds, he seemed a little slow. But he was "willing" and might be a "good batsman."

Just how good a batsman Lyons could become was demonstrated on opening day when he went 3-for-4. He took the collar the next day, but immediately mounted an eight-game hitting streak, and later in April collected 16 hits in 20 at bats. Lyons cooled off after these outbursts, but in May he staged mini-hitting streaks of seven and five games before launching a 19-game skein during which he batted .453 and struck three of his seasonal total of six homers. During this extended streak, his 39 hits included eleven base-on-ball hits. The streak ended on June 18, when pitcher Al Mays of the New York Mets held Lyons hitless in four at bats. The rookie then experienced his worst slump of the season, a four-game drought during which he managed only one hit in 16 at bats.

Lyons was mired in this slump on June 23 when pitcher John "Phenomenal" Smith of Baltimore collared him. A hard-throwing lefty, Smith pitched in 57 games and won 25 in 1887. The next day, the visiting A's faced an even more formidable lefty in Matt Kilroy. The ace of the Baltimore staff, Kilroy was also the league's strikeout king, and in 1887 his 46–20 record led all AA hurlers. But Lyons' single off Kilroy marked the beginning of his unsung hitting streak, which lasted until August 27.

As always, visiting teams tended to lose more often. Given the team's lackluster performance, it was not surprising that Lyons' batting onslaught did little to help matters. The 1887 A's were hard put to win as often as they lost in any diamond environment. For this failure, manager Bancroft was sacked early in June by owner Sharsig, who took charge of the team. Under Bancroft the team's record was 22–25, but under Sharsig the A's were only marginally better, winning 42 of the team's remaining 86 games.

During Lyons' streak, the team won 23, lost 28 and tied one. Moreover, when Lyons began his streak, the A's were mired in a five-game losing streak, and the team won only two of the first eleven games of the streak. Thereafter, Lyons sparked the team to a modest 21–19 resurgence.

Besides playing on a humdrum team, Lyons faced other pressures. Early in the streak manager Sharsig flip-flopped the rookie in the batting order, and not until July was he permanently installed as the number two batter. But Lyons was little affected by such uncertainties or by the pressure of playing on the road. In fact, Lyons hit better on the long road trip at the beginning of his skein than he did during the long homestand that followed. Thus, after opening his streak with single-hit performances off the Baltimore lefties, Lyons smacked two or more hits in 14 of the next 16 road games. As for his two single-hit days, the first came on July 5 at Louisville when Elton "Icebox" Chamberlain held him to a single, and the other came on July 16 when the St. Louis Browns' ace Dave Foutz held him to a double in four at bats.

When the long road swing was interrupted by two home games, Lyons managed to keep his steak alive by singling in each game against Baltimore's Smith and Kilroy. The team returned to Philadelphia on July 21 for a fifteen-game home stand, and Lyons survived the first of these games by doubling in four at bats off Cleveland hurler Hugh "One Arm" Daily.

Lyons' next day's outing was clouded by controversy. In six innings of play he managed only a base-on-balls hit off Cleveland's Mike Morrison. The game ended in the sixth inning after the Cleveland team staged an extended protest over a balk call. The fracas ended when Umpire Mitchell forfeited the game to the A's by a 9–0 score, but under the rules, the batting performances through the six innings went into the record books. Thus Lyons' base-on-balls hit counted and his streak remained intact, at

least for the next 91 years, until the 1968 revisionists made their quixotic ruling to expunge all base-on-ball hits from the 1887 records.

Following that game Lyons had no trouble maintaining his streak over the next 13 home games, although four single-hit games thrust him into a 4-for-19 "slump." The latest of these close calls came on August 8 as the A's ended their homestand, but thereafter Lyons broke loose against the eastern teams by banging 20 hits in his next 37 at bats.

When the A's began another western swing in St. Louis on August 19, Lyons' streak stood at 43 consecutive games. At that time he had hit safely in 21 games since that day in Philadelphia when his only hit had been a base on balls. Now on the afternoon of the 19th, he again benefited from the new scoring rule. Batting against the Browns' Joe Murphy, a marginal player who also served as the baseball editor for a local newspaper, Lyons managed to get two hits in six at bats, but each was a base on balls. Murphy and the resurgent Browns crushed the A's, 22–8.

This was the second and last time that the new scoring rule sustained the streak. Over the next eight games Lyons' 17-for-38 batting powered the A's to a six-game winning streak. The team's streak ended in Cleveland, but as the A's moved into Cincinnati for the last three games of its western swing, Lyons' personal streak stood at 52 games.

It was ironic that Lyons, a native Cincinnatian, should falter in his hometown. It happened on August 27 when the Reds' Tony Mullane, the darling of his team's female fans, shackled Lyons in his five at bats. For good measure, young Elmer Smith collared him the next day to put a decisive ending to the 52-game streak. But it was of no concern to those involved. For neither Lyons nor his tormentors were aware of what had come to pass. Indeed, at no time was the streak mentioned by contemporary observers of the 1887 season. The streak ended as it began, a non-event in a time when baseball's actors were largely innocent of modern statistical notions.

During the remainder of the season Lyons batted close to .400 as the A's finished in fifth place with a 64-69 record. But the 1887 season was a personal triumph for Lyons. His .469 batting average ranked third behind Tip O'Neill's league leading .492 mark and Pete Browning's .472 effort, but Lyons' 284 hits topped all major league batters. What's more, his 118 stolen bases ranked him sixth in the AA, and his .897 fielding average topped all AA third basemen and was bettered only by Jim Whitney in the NL. Had Lyons not committed four errors in his final game, he would have bettered the .900 mark, a lofty achievement at the time. And 1968 revisionists have concluded that Lyons' 255 putouts is the seasonal record for third basemen.

Following his brilliant 1887 season, Lyons played ten seasons in the majors, during which he topped .300 seven times and thrice fielded above .900. During these years he played on four major league teams and was regarded as a solid hitter and fielder. But his reputation was marred by a drinking problem that ended his big league career at age 31. He played briefly in the minors and then settled in West Covington, Kentucky, where he died at age 63 in 1929.

The Revisionists of 1887—After the 1887 campaign, a groundswell of opposition to the scoring of walks as hits pressured the Joint Committee on Rules to rescind the ruling. Leading the assault was Henry Chadwick, the dean of baseball writers. An early supporter of the ruling, Chadwick's opposition followed his survey of the 1887 batting records, which he now denounced as "entirely worthless" and "one of the greatest blunders ever committed...with league statistics." Citing the sky-high batting averages, Chadwick and others demanded "a good overhauling by League and American legislators."

In the face of such opposition, the Joint Committee met in November, 1887 and voted to abolish both the "phantom hit" ruling and the four-strike rule for the 1888 season. Thus in 1888 a batter would again be out after three strikes and a batter drawing a walk would neither get a hit nor be charged with a time at bat. Instead, a pitcher would be charged with an error for issuing a walk. But neither the Joint Committee nor the major league representatives who later voted to rescind the phantom hit rule expressed any regrets over the 1887 experiment. More important, batting averages compiled under the 1887 rules were certified as official in the Reach and Spalding guides.

This easy come–easy go resolution of a major controversy was typical of nineteenth-century rule deliberations. The major league game was still new, and promoters were receptive to the kinds of experiments that would be anathema today. Nor should it be forgotten that such imaginative experiments by officials of yesteryear contributed to establishing the solid foundations of today's major league game.

Glory Denied: the Revisionists of 1968—By the standards of his time, Denny Lyons received his full measure of glory. His seasonal batting, fielding and stolen base performances were properly celebrated and officially enshrined in the official records. That no notice was made of his hitting streak was no denial of glory, since such an achievement was beyond the ken of 1887 statisticians.

His feat was still unrecognized ten years later when Keeler hit in 44 consecutive NL games, and was also ignored. Baseball statisticians of the day were mainly interested in batting averages, hits, stolen bases, fielding averages and such pitching performances as wins and losses and earned run averages. The hitting streaks of Lyons and Keeler lay buried in official records of their times until 1941, when DiMaggio's streak triggered retroactive interest.

Although the historians of 1941 dredged up Keeler's accomplishment, Lyons' feat was undiscovered even though the data were available to a determined researcher. Such data appear in the box scores published in *The Sporting News*, which listed base-on-balls hits without distinction, and in *The Sporting Life*, where the box scores usually, but not always, listed the names of batters who drew walks during games. It is the occasional absence of such listed names that makes it difficult for modern researchers to account for all the base-on-balls hits of 1887.

During his 52-game streak, Lyons batted 233 times and was credited with 103 hits for a .442 batting mark. Among his 103 hits were 18 base-on-ball hits, but only twice was his streak sustained by them.

There is a small possibility that other 1887 hitters, including the AA batters who topped his batting average, might have surpassed Lyons' hitting streak. Tip O'Neill, who played in 123 games and batted .492 with 277 hits, failed to hit in five games during the course of Lyons' midseason streak. Likewise Pete Browning of Louisville, who played in 134 games and batted .471 with 281 hits, failed to hit in four games and sat out another during the course of the streak. It is doubtful that any NL batter matched the streak, because the NL played a shorter schedule and no League hitter matched the lofty averages compiled by O'Neill, Browning and Lyons.

Of course, any researcher aimed at setting the historical record straight on hitting streaks of 1887 runs straight into the 1968 Special Records Committee decision. Not only did the committee expunge Denny Lyons' brilliant effort from the record book, it also pared Tip O'Neill's lofty .492 batting average, officially the highest seasonal mark of any big leaguer, to .435. Worse, Cap Anson, the official NL batting champ of 1887, not only had his .421 average slashed to .347, but was robbed of his title, which the committee retroactively awarded to Sam Thompson of Detroit.

Until the erroneous decisions of the Special Records Committee are overturned, the long history of major league baseball will be blighted by its misguided zeal to make past records fit modern standards. One can only urge baseball historians to unite in common cause to right these wrongs. To this end, historians should chant each day at their breakfast tables this exorcism of wrongheaded revisionists: "Don't meddle with past official records. The lamentable urge to change past records to square with the present is a familiar totalitarian practice. It is anathema to the search for truth and to the integrity of American baseball history."

In Holland, Honk If You Love Baseball

Jay Feldman

When my wife Marti suggested a winter vacation in the Netherlands, I was just a bit nervous. The climate, of course, was one of my concerns: I don't mind it a little chilly, but I'm not keen on real cold weather, and I won't feel especially deprived if I never see snow again.

But the thing that really gave me pause (and I do realize how ridiculous this is going to sound) was the prospect of vacationing in a land where baseball is not a significant part of the culture. It's not that I can't live without baseball for nine days; I'm not that kind of a junkie. It's more that the national pastime is an anchor for me, and during the winter months, I find solace in scanning the sports pages for tidbits of baseball news with their implicit promise that spring is indeed ahead. My concern was that I might feel somewhat adrift, dislocated in a culture that didn't have the summer game as part of its collective experience. I mean, what was I going to look for in those famous Amsterdam flea markets?...there weren't going to be any old baseball gloves to add to my collection.

Nevertheless, Marti, who'd been to Amsterdam twice in the '70s, spoke so highly of the city and the Dutch people that I was persuaded.

I clung to a faint glimmer of hope. The popularity of baseball is increasing throughout Europe now that the game is an Olympic gold medal sport. I'd heard vague rumors of baseball being played in Holland, and I resolved to find it, though I realized that for two reasons this was not going to be easy. First, what Dutch baseball there is would certainly not be played in December. Sec-

ond, we had a full schedule of other activities planned.

Before leaving, I made some preliminary inquiries and turned up nothing. The woman I spoke with at the Netherlands Board of Tourism in Chicago thought she had heard something about baseball in her country but had no idea where to send me.

By good chance, a neighbor of ours had a Dutch houseguest for the holidays. He was very helpful with general hints about the culture and customs of the Netherlands, but when it came to baseball, his response was, "I think a few guys played baseball when I was in high school, but nobody really cared about it."

Oh, well, nobody said it was going to be easy. Our first day in Holland was Tuesday, Dec. 24. We walked through the old, central sections of Amsterdam. I very quickly saw why Marti had been enchanted by the city. The narrow, cobblestone streets, the 17th– and 18th–century architecture, the network of canals, and the friendly, courteous people—almost all of whom speak English—made me quite happy that I'd allowed myself to be persuaded to come here.

Still, there was that little gnawing obsession that I couldn't quite let go of.

We stopped in an antiquarian book store and bought a couple of gifts for friends. I asked the shopkeeper, a pleasant fellow, if he had any books on the American sport of baseball. He looked bemused. "Baseball?" he said, as if he were surprised to hear himself utter the word. (Indeed, it may have been the first time in his life that he spoke it aloud.) "No, I don't think so."

"There is baseball here in the Netherlands, yes?" I asked.

"I think they play someplace over near Utrecht," he

Jay Feldman's article on Roberto Clemente will appear soon in Smithsonian *magazine.*

said with a wave of his hand, and it was clear that this meant the end of discussion on the topic.

I gave up. We weren't planning to visit Utrecht, and I wasn't going to spend any of our precious time on a wild goose chase. Besides, with the little I'd seen so far, I already realized that my anxieties about feeling out of place in this country were groundless. Baseball or no, Holland and I were going to be fast friends. The following day, Wednesday, was Christmas, and while most businesses were closed, the museums were open. We set out early for the Vincent Van Gogh Museum; it was a visit we'd been eagerly anticipating.

On the way to the tram, we walked along the canal street that fronted our hotel, looking in the windows of the closed shops. A few blocks down, I was stopped cold by a bronze statue, about 24 inches high, in the window of a small art gallery. It was a figure in motion, either running or skating. The small sign at the bottom read, "Honkbalspeler (runner)."

We looked the figure over closely. The runner's upper torso strained forward; his right leg extended backwards, bent up at the knee; his left arm was thrust back, bent at the elbow; his right hand touched his left knee. Although it was stylized in the way the sections of bronze were clumped together, the figure expressed the very essence of a runner's all-out striving. And, he was wearing a baseball cap and knickers!

"It's got to be a baseball player," I exclaimed. *Speler*, of course, was "player," close to the German *spieler*. But *honkbal*? I thumbed through my pocket dictionary. Nothing.

"Check the sign on the door, and see when the shop will be open," Marti suggested. As far as I could tell, the gallery was open Tuesday through Sunday. Dec. 26 is also a national holiday in the Netherlands, so the earliest chance would be on Friday the 27th.

Worse luck. Each morning, starting with the 27th, we started out in hopes of finding the gallery open. In spite of the posted hours, it was shut Friday, Saturday and Sunday. Twice a day, on our way out and our way back, I'd take several minutes to look at the mysterious sculpture, hoping to ascertain something more about it, but all I could see was how utterly it captured the act of running (the bases, I was convinced).

Our week was taken up with walking trips through Amsterdam, museum visits, train rides into the countryside and a lot of eating. It was a splendid, much-needed respite, and I must say, except for the frustration of never finding the gallery open, I hardly missed the baseball connection, until....

Monday afternoon, gazing out the window on a train ride through the city, there it suddenly was: an impeccably manicured, emerald-green baseball diamond. I jumped up, grabbed my camera and started snapping away, making sure to get a shot of the "Pirates" billboard outside the ballpark. "I knew it," I said to Marti triumphantly. However much I'd liked Holland to that point, with this discovery I was thoroughly enamored.

On Monday, for the first time, the gallery was true to its posted hours—closed as advertised. I concluded that since it had been shut for the entire Christmas week and would no doubt also be so on New Year's Day, it would therefore be closed on Tuesday, Dec. 31 as well. We were leaving on Jan. 2, and our chances didn't look good. So it was a pleasant surprise when we came by on the morning of the 31st to find the shopkeeper sitting inside. He let us in. I asked to see the *Honkbalspeler* and he brought it from the window. "What sport is this?" I asked.

"It's not the main sport here in Holland," he replied. "In the United States...," he trailed off, clearly at a loss for the word.

"Baseball?" I filled in.

"Yes, that's it. Baseball."

"Can you tell me more about the sculptor?" I didn't ask the price. I didn't want to spoil things just yet.

The dealer took out a large two-volume set of tomes which contained biographical information on all Dutch artists. Our man was Vincent Pieter Semeijn Esser, born in 1914. A sculptor of some note, Esser's bio contained a reference to a photo of one of his works in the back of the book—only important artists' works were so represented, we were told. The dealer flipped to the page indicated, and there was a photo of none other than our *Honkbalspeler (runner)* himself. We were in the presence of greatness!

Up close, the statue was even more remarkable. It said everything about baserunning—the effort, the desire, the abandon. I stroked the bronze and felt the movement in the runner's body.

I couldn't avoid the question any longer. "How much?" He flipped the statue's title card over and there was written "*fl.* 5,500." Five thousand, five hundred guilders. I heard a pop...it was my balloon. I closed my eyes. I didn't have to do an exact calculation to know I was in over my head.

The dealer went to his calculator and punched in some numbers. "About 3,143 American dollars," he said cheerfully. "That's a good price."

"Yes, I'm sure it is," I said. "But it's more than we are prepared to spend." I asked if I could take a couple of pictures instead. No problem. On our way out, the dealer mentioned another gallery in the neighborhood that specialized in sports art.

We walked over to the other gallery. Among the depictions of skiing, soccer, American football, tennis and the rest, was a handful of baseball paintings and one small bronze sculpture of a pitcher in his windup, but they all paled in comparison with Esser's *Honkbalspeler (runner)*.

I did, however, find the lead I'd been hoping for. In response to my questions about baseball in Holland, the shopkeeper gave me the phone number of the Royal Dutch Baseball and Softball Organization office in

Haarlem. Finally, I'd cracked the code.

The office was getting ready to close for New Year's, but I was given the phone number of Marco Stoovelaar, an Amsterdam journalist who acts as official scorer and publicist for the Tas Detach Pirates, the club whose park we'd seen from the train.

From Marco, I learned that baseball was brought to Holland in 1911 by one J. Grase, a physical education instructor who had seen and played the sport in the U.S. Dutch baseball is organized on a club system: 300 clubs (30,000 members) sponsor between three and ten teams each, starting with peanut ball (t-ball) for five-year olds. The highest level of play is the 10-team *Hoofdklasse* or major league, which plays a 45-game (3 games a week) schedule between mid-April and the end of September, culminating in the championship Holland Series, which the Pirates have won the past two years. Each *Hoofdklasse* team is allowed two American players—usually guys who've played AA or AAA ball in the States.

Marco also reminded me that Win Remmerswaal, a Dutchman, had appeared in 22 games in relief for the Boston Red Sox in 1979-80, and told me to keep my eye on Rikkert Faneyte, a pitcher in the San Francisco Giants' minor league organization, and Robert Eenhoorn, a first baseman in the New York Yankees' chain.

And, oh yes, *honk* means base.

Marco invited us over to his brother Ronald's house the next evening, our last in Holland. Ronald is the Pirates' catcher and a member of the national team. We spent a lovely evening with the Stoovelaar brothers, their parents, grandmothers and girlfriends. The main topic of conversation was, of course, baseball. We promised that our next visit would be during the season and that we'd take a trip over to Haarlem to see the *honkbal* museum.

My Winter Vacation: Went to the Netherlands. Had a wonderful time. In addition to everything else, made some new baseball friends and saw a sculpture, the very essence of baserunning. Small world.

Musial kicks...and delivers....

In his Hall-of-Fame baseball career, St. Louis Cardinals slugger Stan Musial, who began as a minor league pitcher, actually got to face one batter.

Playing the fifth-place Chicago Cubs on the last day of the 1952 season, Cardinals Manager Eddie Stanky moved rookie Harvey Haddix from the mound to the outfield and brought Musial in to pitch to hot-hitting Frankie Baumholtz, who finished second to Stan the Man for the NL batting championship that year.

Baumholtz, a lefthanded-batting outfielder, promptly turned around to hit righthanded against Musial.

"I told my manager [Phil Cavaretta] that I had never hit righthanded in my life, but that if they were going to bring Musial in to pitch to me, I was going to do it," says Baumholtz. "Stanky had advertised the day before that Musial was going to pitch, and 20,000 or so fans showed up. Usually, you'd only get a couple hundred or so for two second-division teams playing on the last day of the season."

Despite hitting righthanded, Baumholtz belted a line drive off the leg of Cardinal third baseman Solly Hemus. "It ate Solly alive and just smashed into his knee," remembers Haddix. "Somehow, they called it an error. If ever there was a clean hit, that was it."

"And it was probably the hardest liner I ever hit," says Baumholtz with a laugh.

—Steve Stout

Stardom...and then out!

In 1945, Tony Cuccinello batted .308 and was edged out for the American League batting title by a mere point (.309 by Snuffy Stirnweiss.)

In the 1947 World Serie,s there were three sparkling achievements: Al Gionfriddo's great catch of Joe DiMaggio's drive; Bill Bevens' near-miss of a first-ever World Series no-hitter, and Cookie Lavagetto's game-winning double that ruined that no-hit bid.

Yet, Cuccinello never played another season in the majors, nor did the Fall Classic stars, Gionfriddo, Bevens, and Lavagetto.

Understandable in Cuccinello's case. He was 37 years old, and was probably only playing because of wartime conditions. But Gionfriddo was 25, Bevens was 30, and Lavagetto was 33.

—Jack Keeley

The 1884 Altoona Unions

Jerry Jaye Wright

The year 1884 marked the inaugural season of the ephemeral Union Association League, a league which challenged the baseball establishment of the period and its reserve rule, and whose flaccid administrative practices, revolving franchises, and caliber of play leaves its claim to have been a major league open to question. Equally suspect were several of the Union's franchise cities, one of which was Altoona, Pennsylvania.

Altoona was the smallest city awarded a Union franchise; a selection made purely for the benefit of the League, and not because Altoona was on a par with professional baseball's other major league cities.

The Union Association was organized in Pittsburgh at a meeting of the Union Association of Base Ball Clubs, September 12, 1883. At the Association's third meeting, December 18, 1883, in Philadelphia, Henry Van Noye Lucas, a wealthy St. Louis real estate and railroad tycoon with a fanatical interest in baseball, was elected league president by acclamation. As league president, the 26-year-old Lucas became the guiding force behind the Union Association. He assembled a strong team for St. Louis, the Maroons, and gave freely of his time and financial assistance to the Association and a number of other clubs, including Altoona.

By 1883, Altoona had established a rich amateur baseball tradition, which was showing signs of growing into professionalism. In March, 1883, The Altoona Base Ball Club was formed, and it competed independently with other town clubs across the state and in the Inter-State League. The club was well organized and was supported financially by non-playing local businessmen. Total club membership was twenty-two, including twelve players and team captain and player-manager, Harry C. Fisher.

Which league?—By the close of the 1883 season, club organizers were ambitiously looking forward to the next year. During a four-month span, the Altoona Base Ball Club joined, or considered membership in, three different leagues. In November, 1883, the club applied and was accepted for membership into the Inter-State Base Ball Association, a league consisting of eight teams throughout Pennsylvania, New Jersey, and Delaware. At the Association's January 2, 1884, meeting in Philadelphia, the Altoona organization received some unexpected administrative clout when club secretary Edwin Curtis was elected league president. Curtis' new position generated public excitement in Altoona and club founder Arthur Dively raised additional capital for the recruitment of skilled players.

On Friday, February 1, 1884, while the Inter-State Association met at the Girard House in Philadelphia to vote on additional club memberships and to finalize playing schedules, the upstart Union Association was building momentum. By now it was clear the Unions had no intention of honoring the player contracts of other leagues. Instead, under Lucas' direction, the Association virtually declared open season on other leagues' players' stating that the Union "does not favor the arbitrary reserve rule, which makes the player almost the slave of the club." As a means to ward off the threat posed by the newly organized Union Association, the National League and

Dr. Jerry Jaye Wright is Associate Professor of Sport History, Department of Exercise and Sport Science, Penn State—Altoona campus.

American Association banded together to establish the Eastern League, designed to serve as a minor league that would keep players bound to the two major league organizations. While the Eastern League probably served its intended purpose, it quickly marked the demise of the Inter-State Association, as several clubs immediately jumped to the Eastern League, leaving only Altoona and clubs from Lancaster and Chester, Pennsylvania and Elizabeth, New Jersey. Suddenly, all their grand plans for 1884 had collapsed, and the Altoona Base Ball Club faced a dilemma. Either join the Eastern League or return to the independent format of the previous season.

On the evening of February 4, 1884, a special club meeting was called at the law office of Arthur Dively to determine the club's direction. Mr. Dively and other club members expressed interest in following their Inter-State Association counterparts into the Eastern League. But Secretary Curtis' interest was in the rival Unions. During the meeting, he advocated membership in the Union Association, stating, "Altoona is 122 miles from Pittsburgh, has a population of 25,000, and is the best base ball city in Pennsylvania outside of Philadelphia, and the average attendance at ball games last season was 1,600 . . . the Club has signed several top players for this season and the city is expecting some good play."

Secretary Curtis' argument was apparently unconvincing, as club members voted to seek membership in the Eastern League. But their application was denied. The setback prompted a second meeting on the evening of February 9, 1884, to decide the club's fate. During the lengthy meeting, two decisions were unanimously agreed upon: to make application for Union Association membership, and to reorganize the club as the Altoona Base Ball Association, Limited. Formal application, along with the $100 application fee, was submitted to Union Association secretary Warren White, in Washington, D.C., February 11, 1884.

To the Unions—Altoona's Union Association application may have been the break president Lucas was looking for. The Unions had been trying unsuccessfully to place a franchise in Pittsburgh to serve as a stopover connecting the UA's eastern and western cities. Despite Altoona's small population and hinterland location, Lucas saw the city's potential for fulfilling this need. Baseball was popular in Altoona, but even more important in 1884, Altoona was a railroad hub connecting eastern and western cities. The frequent passing of trains with Union Association teams would no doubt promote and stimulate interest in baseball and the new league. On March 2, 1884, Union Association secretary White telegraphed Mr. Curtis in Altoona that his club was accepted for membership and would join seven other clubs: Baltimore, Boston, Chicago, Cincinnati, Philadelphia, St. Louis, and Washington, D.C., to form an eight team league. However, the local media failed to report that Altoona's selection was

contingent only, based on four "yes" votes with St. Louis and Cincinnati "non-committal," and subject to rescission at the spring meeting in Cincinnati, March 17, 1884.

Contingent membership did not seem to dampen the spirit of the club or of Altoonans as excitement ran high over having major league baseball in the city. Local newspapers praised the work of club president William Ritz and secretary Curtis, and the community nicknamed their team the Altoona Pride. But there were accounts of criticism that Altoona had made a critical mistake detrimental to the city's young baseball heritage. In a newspaper editorial, at least one staunch supporter of organized baseball expressed reservation as to the caliber of play of the new league. Additionally, under the Union Association charter, member teams were barred from competing against professional clubs outside the Association. Also, in light of Association policy that home teams pay visiting clubs $75, or a percentage of the gate if larger for expenses, it was felt the Altoona Club had limited its playing and revenue opportunities with restricted play within the Union Association.

Nonetheless, the Altoona club showed little or no concern for the criticism or for the continuous rumors that they would be dropped from the UA, and rapidly began preparation for the upcoming season. The club's reorganization foresight helped to alleviate some of the financial burden, as incorporation and charter guidelines allowed the club to issue stock at one dollar per share. Stock shares were available to the pubic, but the majority of shares were purchased by local businessmen.

On March 8, 1884, League President Lucas arrived in Altoona, at which time he met with club president Ritz, secretary Curtis, and several shareholders and assured them of Altoona's Union Association membership. Further assurance came during the meeting when Lucas offered his personal investment of $2,500, and agreed to influence local businesses to purchase stock shares. After little discussion, the club graciously accepted Lucas' investment by majority vote. Further revenues were generated through commutation tickets, a $5 pass which enabled the bearer to attend twenty-five home games. Scheduling also helped the club's financial structure. Altoona's first seven games were played on the road, thus eliminating the $75 per game payment to visiting clubs.

By mid-March, as a result of investors, the Altoona Base Ball Club, Limited, had amassed over $5,000 in capital, and appeared solvent. Altoona was ready. The only concern now was the Union's spring meeting. On Monday, March 17, 1884, the Union Association met behind closed doors at the Gibson House in Cincinnati. There, the rumors of Altoona's not being accepted were put to rest as its membership was confirmed. Boston also received confirmation, rounding out the eight club circuit.

Handsome, but weak—The Altoona club was one of six teams privileged to open the Union Association season on

the future home of the Dodgers was still a sovereign city, not yet a tempting appendage to New York and its Tammany overlords. Like the newly-born Willie, pro ball was in its infancy. Only a year before his birth, the National Association of Professional Baseball Players had been organized in Collier's Cafe in Manhattan. Soon, whole teams of ballplayers could earn several thousands of dollars a year.

Salaries like that may seem ludicrous by today's mind-boggling standards, but in Willie's time a dollar bought lots of groceries and other of life's essentials. To youthful Americans, particularly those from poorer families (Keeler Sr. was a trolley switchman), playing baseball seemed a splendid way to earn a living. Certainly it was better than toiling in a mill, or carrying hods, or digging coal in the bowels of Pennsylvania.

"When professional baseball was first organized in the 1870s," writes Stephan A. Riess, "the average manufacturing employee worked about ten and a half hours a day, six days a week." Facing a 63-hour work week, it was small wonder that baseball-happy kids like Willie Keeler chose pro ball for their careers. And when did young men in lowly, confining occupations ever hear the cheers of the crowd as they did in the National Pastime?

When Willie was learning the three R's at P.S. 26 in Brooklyn, and no doubt perfecting the crafty dexterities of his swing, it took eight balls to earn a walk; home plate was forty-five feet from the pitcher's box; the ball was dead, the fields were scrubby, and umpiring was often a hazardous occupation. In 1888 Willie quit school to play ball as a pitcher and third baseman with the semi-pro Brooklyn Acmes. His gross income was $1.50 per game.

After sharpening his skills on the sandlots of the City of Churches, in 1892 Keeler hied himself to the Plainfield, N.J. Crescents semi-pros at a 33-$\frac{1}{3}$ percent raise. He got $2 per game. Then, at what must have seemed like a bonanza to young Willie, Binghamton of the Eastern League grabbed him at a $90 per month salary.

His first pro appearance was on June 6, 1892, when he—a left-handed thrower— played shortstop and went 1-for-3 as Binghamton beat Syracuse 4–2. We have no record of where Willie placed his hit, or of the latent anxieties of the Syracuse players. But as the season progressed, players and fans alike realized that Willie was no ordinary athlete. Not only was he uncommonly adept at getting on base, but he could play the outfield, short, second, and third. In sum, Keeler was a .373 godsend to the Binghamton club and its fans. But not for long. The New York Giants soon bought him for $800. After playing fourteen games at third in 1893, he was peddled to Brooklyn, again for $800, after which, in 1894, he was traded to the Baltimore Orioles, then a National League club, in a deal crucial for Willie and baseball. Soon he and his Oriole cohorts became a baseball legend.

In a recent interview, Billy Herman, the scrappy old Cubs and Dodgers second baseman and Hall of Famer, labeled today's ball players, "a bunch of pantywaists." Plainly, if he'd been around in the 1890's, Herman would have approved of the Orioles. For not only could Baltimore play superb baseball, but their waists were anything but pantied.

Indeed, to call a ball player an "Old Oriole" is to bestow upon him one of the game's ultimate compliments—provided you don't dwell on ethical behavior. A club devoid of high-minded principles, the Orioles would beat you not only by superior skills, but by bending the rules, a sure temptation in a time when baseball fielded only one umpire. Here is the great Honus Wagner describing, with tongue only partly in cheek, a potential inside-the-park homer he smacked against the Orioles.

"Jack Doyle gave me the hip at first; Heinie Reitz almost killed me when I rounded second; Hughie Jennings tripped me at shortstop; and when I got to third John McGraw was waiting for me with a shotgun." Wagner settled for a triple.

Manager Ned Hanlon's squad of talented delinquents numbered seventeen men: five are in the Hall of Fame—John McGraw, Hughie Jennings, Wilbert Robinson, Joe Kelley, and Willie Keeler. Of that celebrated group McGraw, whose deserved and bellicose nickname was "Muggsy," set the example of dead-ball era strategy, spiced with hooligan play. It included the hit-and-run, the squeeze, bunting (a decaying skill in our time), and other tactics comprised in the designation, "inside baseball." For ability and performance Keeler, usually batting second, and now primarily a right fielder, was without question the best of the Orioles.

In Keeler's time bats had thicker handles than they have today, and he made the most of that design. With remarkable mastery he used not only the power end of the bat but, when pitched close, he also used the thick handle to pop the ball where the infielders weren't. Years later McGraw said of Willie, "No one who ever batted a baseball was more adept at placing a hit than Keeler...His skill was uncanny. He seemed to sense what the opposing fielders would do, and he had the skill to 'cross' them."

As for Willie's fielding, writer Fred Lieb quotes his former editor, Jim Price, a Baltimorean who saw Keeler play in the Orioles' prime days. Price "...told of a catch Keeler made in Washington. He ripped open his arm to the elbow by thrusting it through a barbed-wire fence, but caught the ball with his bare hand."

And according to Lieb, Chicago writer Hugh Fullerton "...told of seeing Keeler make another amazing catch...Right field...was rough and reedy, and back of it was a high fence...Inside the fence sloped at an angle of 65 degrees, though it was straight on the outside. With two runners on base, Chick Stahl of Boston hit a long fly to right, which looked like the winning clout...Keeler, running like a scared rabbit, mounted the fence, higher and higher, and with a final thrust caught the ball just as it was clearing the fence...the little outfielder's momentum was so great that he ran for another fifteen feet on top of the fence before falling...to the street below." The umpire ruled the catch legal.

Old Oriole, indeed!

Baltimore won three straight pennants (1894–1896) as Keeler compiled the first of his string of great stats. His batting averages in the Oriole years were .371, .377, .386, .424, .385. (That .424 in 1897 is based on *Total Baseball*'s 239 hits in 564 at-bats. These are reasonably defensible numbers, but we must remember that when we venture into the swampy ground of early statistics, we may never know the exact truth. Even using the other available statistics, Keeler's mark was not surpassed until Ty Cobb collected 248 hits in 1911.)

Hanlon switched to Brooklyn in 1899, taking Willie and other Orioles with him. There Keeler continued his slicing, chopping, and blooping to average .353 in his four Brooklyn years. When added to his Oriole marks, he compiled a string of batting averages rarely approached in over one hundred years of big league ball. And he added three more 200-hit seasons to make eight in a row in that department.

Willie's lifetime average is .341, based on the most recent edition of *Total Baseball*. That's higher than the BA's of Bill Terry, George Sisler, Lou Gehrig, Al Simmons and many other great hitters.

Although he was slowing down by the time he got to the American League, Willie still hit over .300 in four of his seven years as a Highlander/Yankee (1903–1909). Imagine what Willie, in the embrace of agents, lawyers, and tax gurus, would earn today! But let's end the stats-chronicle with the two of which Keeler was proudest—although, unfortunately, there are questions about the accuracy of these numbers from so long ago.

Contemporary records show that in 8,591 at-bats during his nineteen years in the majors, Keeler struck out only 36 times! To an innocent eye, they also indicate that for thirteen years in a row, 1897–1909, he didn't strike out at all! If those records were accurate, they would put him second on the all-time list for fewest strikeouts per game with a .019 average, just behind Joe Sewell's .016.

But we now know that the zero strikeouts credited to Willie from 1897–1909 are not an actual tally, butthe results o no records having been kept on his K's over those years. Even for a hitter of Willie's caliber, it is difficult to accept that he *never* struck out, and serious baseball scholars don't. Pete Palmer reminds us that Bob Davids, a SABR founding father, has been researching Keeler's SO numbers, but a definite tally is proving elusive.

Joe Sewell was a master at putting the ball in play, but even he never went for a season or more with no strikeouts. Sewell's lowest was three (1930 and 1932).

Though Keeler was paid well for playing—as much as $10,000 a season in uninflated bucks—he insisted that mainly he played ball for the sheer love of it. Said Willie, "I'm thinking of those suckers, the owners, paying me for playing ball. Why, I'd pay my way to get into their parks if that was the only way I had to get in a ball game."

Hyperbole aside, the statement rings true. This, despite the fact that before the advent of today's strong players' union, free agentry, restrictions on trading, and other contractual benefits, players were under the almost complete domination of owners. For Willie Keeler, a man who loved baseball with a child's artless passion, the game was at the center of his life. And therein lay the source of his post-baseball misfortune.

The great poet Robert Frost has written that each of us must find something to stave off "the black and utter chaos" that life can become without a dominant motive to nourish it. The enervating boredom, the aimlessness, the often erratic behavior we see in those who have no meaningful purpose in life validates Frost's insight. So does the evidence of Keeler's last years, a time when what was the center of his being—playing a game learned as a child— had vanished. Certainly his retirement in Brooklyn was in stark contrast to his fabled playing career.

Released after 39 games with minor league Toronto in 1911, Keeler had nothing in his life that could replace the challenge and splendor of his playing days. It might have been better if he had remained in baseball, perhaps as a coach or scout. But he tried each in 1915 and failed. Not a commanding type, he didn't want to manage. (When he'd been sought out for the Highlander managing job in 1908, he ducked out of the Philadelphia hotel where the team was staying so that owner Frank Farrell couldn't find him.)

He retired from baseball reputed to have saved $100,000; indeed, he was called the "Brooklyn Millionaire." Whether Keeler was ill-advised, or conned by sharpsters laying in wait for ingenuous types, is unknown. But his "unwise speculation [in real estate] wrecked all that the little fellow had built up...he was dead broke...With his weakened heart, and dubious financial condition little Willie Keeler's last days were anything but happy ones," wrote J.C. Kofoed in *The Sporting News* after Willie's death.

In a prescient article written just before Willie died, *The Sporting News* also stated, "The world might have used him better than it has. He deserved more of a reward than he seems to have received, but nothing ever can take from him the reputation which he made for himself with his bat."

A *New York Tribune* editorial a day after Willie's death compared him to Napoleon, another man of small stature and large achievement, in "...swiftness and accuracy of observation, a poise permitting of instant allocation of plan and execution."

(In plainer words, a man who "hit 'em where they ain't.")

And, added the writer, "Willie Keeler had all those qualities, and while he had them he was a great athlete. That he ended in failure and died poor but proves the case as did Waterloo."

Keeler received a $5,500 gift from the major leagues in 1921, and though welcome, the money was no panacea. Finally penniless, a bachelor living alone in little more than a shack, he was seemingly forgotten. In 1922, when George Sisler assaulted Willie's 45 straight (or, if you will, 44 in a single season) with 41 in a row—again, without today's media commotions—nobody thought of interviewing Keeler about it.

Bedridden and ill with heart trouble on the last day of 1922, Keeler knew he was in a losing game; yet he told his brother that he wanted to make it into the new year. That night some family and friends dropped in to see him; just before midnight they stepped outside to hear the Brooklyn church bells ring in the New Year. When they returned there was Willie sitting up, triumphantly ringing in 1923 with the hand-bell at his bedside.

On New Year's Day, January 1, 1923, the Old Oriole (Hall of Fame, 1939), a great player, a diamond original marvelously adept at baseball but at little else in the demanding adult world around him—a world whose often disheartening, sometimes bloody games aren't played on a field before adoring crowds—Wee Willie Keeler died at fifty.

Almost forgotten in life, in death Willie experienced a kind of resurrection. Tributes and flowers poured into his shanty home from baseball notables; high brass from every New York club attended his funeral; Old Orioles McGraw, Hanlon, Kelley, Robinson, and Kid Gleason were pallbearers. McGraw kneeled, prayed, and wept at his coffin.

Willie Keeler is buried at Calvary Cemetery in Brooklyn, but his name and his record are forever with us. A mite of a man, he stands tall with the titans of the game. And the remembrance of him—a remembrance kept green even in the minds of kids who quote his admirable counsel about how to get on base—is part of baseball's golden legacy.

Thanks, guys

Larry Jackson hurled for the Chicago Cubs in 1963 when they were 82–80, and he compiled a losing slate of 14–18. The next year the Cubbies slumped to 76–86, but Jackson's won–lost record improved considerably to 245–11. One would naturally assume that Jackson's 1964 ERA must have been vastly superior to that of 1963. On the contrary, in 1963, he gave up only 2.55 runs per nine innings, and the next year, he surrendered 3.14. Clearly, the "poorer" team backed him with consistent offense, while the "better" club simply didn't hit behind him.

—Jack Keeley

Could Franklin P. Adams write a poem about this?

In the first game of a doubleheader played on July 8, 1934 in Fenway Park, the Athletics' Bob Johnson stepped to the plate in the seventh inning. Boston hurler Hank Johnson wound up and pitched to Bob, who hit the ball to center field. It was caught on the fly by a fellow named Roy Johnson. The three Johnsons made the pitch, the hit, and the putout.—From information in the Boston Globe, *July 9, 1934.*

—Joe Dittmar

"Doc" Powers' Shocking End

Joe Dittmar

It was April 12, 1909, and in Philadelphia, Benjamin F. Shibe was about to open the first of a new generation of baseball arenas. Unlike other ballparks of the day, Shibe Park was constructed almost entirely of concrete and steel, making it virtually fireproof and indestructible while rendering knothole viewers an extinct breed. This was a half-million dollar structure, described as the largest and most ornate monument to the sport in the country. Highly touted was the fact that each row of seats rose 14 inches, permitting a clear view even for those sitting behind female patrons wearing "peachbasket" hats. In addition, the upper pavilion was a cantilever construction enabling virtually every seat to have an "unobstructed" view of the action. There were 10,000 folding chairs in the grandstand, an innovation for outdoor parks, available for 50 cents each. All totaled there were 23,000 seats and room for another 17,000 to stand, mostly in front of the outfield walls, where the ground was especially banked for that purpose. Shibe, in anticipation of the largest crowd ever to witness a baseball game in this country, had both the left and right outfields roped off to allow those without seats to also view the festivities. Beneath the bleachers were two parking garages, each large enough to accommodate 200 "machines."

The Athletics had even been scheduled to open their season two days early to allow other team's players and dignitaries to attend this colossal event. (The New York club did visit Washington for the only other game that day.)

Directions to the new park were printed in the newspapers and the weatherman cooperated by predicting a mild, sunny day for the 3 o'clock inaugural.

At noon, the twelve entry gates were opened, allowing many who had been waiting for hours to begin filling the edifice. The First and Third Regiment Bands provided non-stop music from 1:00 to 2:30 PM while fans stampeded their way through the turnstiles, tearing garments and crushing one another. After all the seats filled, the rest of the crowd was herded behind the outfield ropes. Around 2 o'clock, sensing a dwindling availability of tickets, thousands still on the streets began uncontrollable rushes on the main gates, forcing the police to halt further entry. *The Public Ledger* estimated 15,000 were left outside to batter, bang, yell and surge around the four sides of the park. Despite several attempts to storm the gates, attendance was halted at less than capacity. In addition to 30,162 paid, there were several thousand complimentary attendees and an estimated 3,000 who watched from the rooftops, porches and windows of homes behind the outfield walls. Included in the congregation were Philadelphia Mayor Reyburn, Ban Johnson, president of the American League, many Phillies players, and magnates from other teams. For 25 cents, fans lined up seven to ten rows deep in the outfields, and strings of dangling legs spread across the twelve-foot high concrete walls as well as the scoreboard, rendering it useless. Despite the fact that this was the opening day of the 1909 season, the game itself became secondary to the revelry.

At 2:30, both bands marched onto the field and played "America" while all those in the park stood and sang in an emotional show of patriotism. Then, led by Ben Shibe and Ban Johnson, both bands and members of both squads

Joe Dittmar is the author of Baseball's Benchmark Boxscores: Summaries of the Record-Setting Games.

Doc Powers

Veteran southpaw Eddie Plank took the hill for the Athletics. When he'd been a rookie, Powers had helped him through some rough times. Doc often calmed the high-strung Plank with his familiar chant: "Work hard, old boy, work hard." They were friends off the field, too, and Doc even became Plank's personal physician. Powers was a gentleman with a sunny disposition, respected and well liked.

The game itself was far less exciting than the preliminaries. Plank led the A's to an easy 8-1 victory. It was a fitting ending to a magnificent day.

The throng left the park amid much celebration but in the home team's clubhouse the atmosphere was a bit more reserved. Powers, who had experienced intense abdominal pain starting around the seventh inning, collapsed. He was rushed by ambulance to Northwest General Hospital where he was diagnosed as having "acute gastritis." Several newspapers reported the probable cause was the few cheese sandwiches he had eaten before or during the game coupled with the excitement of the day. The attending physicians stated that he would be back in uniform within a few days.

The following day, Tuesday, April 13, doctors said his situation was worse than expected and that it might take several days before they could diagnose his ailment. They declared there were no indications of serious complications.

That night however, Powers took a turn for the worse and opiates were administered. When they proved unsuccessful in alleviating his excruciating pain, immediate surgery was performed at 1:00 AM Wednesday. The surgeon did not paint a bright picture. He announced the problem as "intussusception of the intestines" meaning that the intestine had folded inside of itself. Blood vessels became strangled, creating a gangrenous state, forcing the removal of at least 12 inches of his bowel. Shockingly, Powers was given just one chance in five to survive.

The report from the hospital of Thursday, April 15, listed Doc as stable, but not yet out of danger. On April 20, *The North American* headline rang out, "POWERS HAS RELAPSE; CONDITION PERILOUS". Symptoms of deadly peritonitis had developed and Powers was forced to undergo a second operation, which left him in a greatly weakened state.

On April 23, with Doc Powers still fighting for his life, an ominous telegram was released by Connie Mack proclaiming his purchase of catcher Paddy Livingston from Indianapolis of the American Association.

On April 25, having undergone still a third operation, Powers was near death. The hospital's staff of physicians had used every known procedure in an effort to save Doc's life but were now resigned to the inevitable conclusion. Stimulants, which had been freely prescribed, were withdrawn, allowing nature to take its unrelenting course. Doc was administered the Last Sacrament, while his wife, Florence, joined in the responses. Doc

paraded to the flagpole in deep center field for the raising of Old Glory and a singing of "The Star Spangled Banner". At 3 o'clock, as the first Boston batter approached the plate, the A's 38-year-old veteran backstop, Mike Powers, walked to the grandstand and caught Mayor Reyburn's ceremonial first-ball toss. Powers had been with the A's since their birth and was the only player in today's starting lineup who also started in the club's first major league game eight years before. Doc represented an unusual combination of talents. He acquired his nickname because he was one of the few legitimate doctors to play major league baseball while simultaneously practicing medicine. Powers was a weak hitter but his defense, his throwing arm and his leadership made him Connie Mack's choice to catch the first game in Shibe Park.

was conscious throughout and, clasping the priest's hand, thanked him for his kindness. Meanwhile, scores of fans gathered outside the hospital, hoping for a spark of positive news.

The merciful end came at 9:14 AM on April 26, exactly two weeks after that glorious opening of Shibe Park. Minutes before expiring, he shouted "I've got no pulse, no pulse!" Doc knew, as well as the attending staff, that the end had arrived. As he died, Florence also collapsed. The *Philadelphia Inquirer* wrote: "DOC POWERS CALLED BY THE INEXORABLE UMPIRE." The *Philadelphia Record* more aptly described the situation with: "DEATH RELIEVES CATCHER POWERS."

Flags at all major league parks were ordered to half-mast. Letters and telegrams of sympathy poured into the Athletics' office as Connie Mack left his team to console Mrs. Powers and assist her with the funeral arrangements. Mack and Powers had been close friends. They had much in common. Both were Irish Catholics from Massachusetts, and each had worn the tools of ignorance as players.

Final arrangements were to include a modest viewing at the home of family friend George Flood, but no one was quite prepared for the volume of public outpouring.

Dittmar

Starting at 7:30 PM, thousands of mourners lined several city blocks for one last look at the much loved Powers. Extra police were summoned to maintain a swift, orderly procession of the throng that filed through the Flood parlor, covered with an avalanche of floral arrangements. Finally, at 3:00 AM, the doors were closed, leaving many disappointed. At 5:00 AM, the house was again opened to hundreds more who began to line the streets. When the doors were again closed at 9:30 AM, another 500 mourners were disappointed. Newspapers estimated that in excess of 10,000 people had viewed the body during the two sessions.

On the day of the funeral, April 29, the Athletics were scheduled to play in Washington. With league permission, both teams voted to postpone the game and the entire Washington squad as well as the Athletics traveled to Philadelphia to show their respect. The Phillies and the Brooklyn Dodgers, who were still in town, also attended.

The funeral procession followed the few city blocks to St. Elizabeth's Church. Carrying the casket were Eddie Plank, Harry Davis, Ira Thomas, Jack Coombs, Simon Nicholls and Danny Murphy, followed by Doc's widow, on the arm of Connie Mack, and her three young daughters. Along the way, opportunists sold photos of the Athletics' catcher to the thousands who lined the pavements. When the cortege approached the church, thirty policemen were needed to break through the swarm of people outside. It, too, had been closed earlier when mourners packed it almost to the point of suffocation.

More than a year later, at the urging of Connie Mack, a benefit game was arranged for Florence Powers and her three young daughters. The eastern American League teams, Philadelphia, Boston, Washington and New York, were af-

TICKETS

"DOC" POWERS' DAY

THURSDAY JUNE 30
—
FOR THE BENEFIT OF THE WIDOW AND CHILDREN OF THE "ATHLETICS" LAMENTED CATCHER

BASEBALL AND SPECIAL EVENTS

FAN

LEST WE FORGET.

By McGurk.

Philadelphia Record/Dittmar

DEAR FRIEND:—
The sad death of Dr. Power, over a year ago, took from our midst one who was esteemed by all. He was loyal, kindly and faithful in all of his duties, a fine disposition that only saw the bright side of things and the good in life. To Base Ball he was the *to* that was in him, and he died a Martyr to the game.

His one thought was for the happiness of his wife and three little ones, and the future of his children. Almost his last words were, "I am not thinking of myself, I am thinking of my wife and little ones."

The "Athletic" Club wishes that his one great desire shall be accomplished,—that his widow shall not want, and that his children will be given the education he had planned for them. For that purpose, Thursday, June 30th was left an open date in the Eastern schedule of the American League, to be known as "Doc. Powers' Day." All of the receipts of this day will be turned over to the widow. We want this fund to be a grand one, and trust we may have your help in this worthy cause by the presence of yourself and your friends. Very sincerely yours,

Pm. 5-21-10 Connie Mack

Mr Aubrey R Morris

Delta, York Co.

Box 35   Penna

THROWING FOR ACCURACY (From catcher's position to a target on second base)—Pat Donahue (Philadelphia).

NOVELTY EVENT: From catcher's position, throwing to second base beneath a 6' bar at pitchers mound—Jimmy Austin (NY).

RUNNING THE BASES (Home to Home)—Eddie Collins (Philadelphia), 14.2 seconds.

RELAY BASERUNNING—Barry, Coombs, Collins, Rath (Philadelphia), 14.4 seconds.

LONG DISTANCE THROW—Harry Hooper (Boston), 356'4".

100 YARD DASH—Jimmy Austin (NY), 10.6 seconds.

forded a day off and most of the players from each team participated, meaning nearly 100 players graced Shibe Park on Thursday, June 30, 1910.

More than a month before, preparations were being made, invitations being mailed. Mack had a special postcard printed and sent to many Powers admirers. Newspaper advertisements urged fans and humanitarians to contribute to the "Mike Powers Day" with all proceeds earmarked for the education of his children.

Publicized as the highlights of the day were the pre-game field events, throwing, running, batting competitions and a special "novelty event." A band donated their time, and everyone, including Messrs. Mack and Shibe, Charles Ebbets, and even the mayor, paid their way into the stadium. Newspapers estimated from 10,000 to 15,000 turned out.

Just before the events were to begin, Connie Mack was cajoled out of the dugout to receive a huge bouquet of roses at home plate from Eddie Plank. They were in recognition of Connie's efforts to bring this altruistic day to fruition. It was the first time Philadelphians ever saw Mack out of the dugout and they responded with tumultuous applause. Seated behind the Athletics' dugout, dressed in black, was Florence Powers, who was asked to draw winning program numbers for season's passes to the remaining Phillies and A's games.

The field event participation was serious, although Washington's ballplayer–clown, Germany Schaefer, entertained the crowd by entering most of the events and serving as announcer, timekeeper and judge whenever possible. A summary of the contests and winners:

BUNTING & RUNNING TO FIRST BASE—Harry Lord (Boston), 3.2 seconds.

100 YARD DASH (Over 200 lbs.)—Jake Stahl (Boston), 10.8 seconds.

FUNGO HITTING—Jimmy Dygert (Philadelphia).

The only damper put on the day was an injury to the A's Harry Davis when he inadvertently walked in front of Walter Johnson during the fungo hitting contest. Davis walked smack into the swinging bat of Johnson and was leveled by a blow to the forehead. Somehow he managed to stagger to the bench for the balance of the afternoon.

Due to the number of participants, these events took almost four hours, leaving little patience for an actual game. But as promised, the tired players hastily took the field. The "Picked-Team" consisted of over 70 players. Even the Boston mascot, Jerry McCarthy, batted. Each inning, there were wholesale lineup changes, making a box score ludicrous. Consequently, only a line score was kept and after about an hour, everyone had had enough. By the time a local amateur umpire declared the home team victors, a large part of the crowd had gone home.

								R	H	E
Picked Team	3	0	0	0	0	0	-	3	10	4
Athletics	0	0	4	0	0	0	-	4	12	2

Connie Mack and Ben Shibe were radiant with joy at the day's success. When the receipts were finally tallied, nearly $8,000 had been raised in Powers' name. The *Philadelphia Press* called it baseball's greatest tribute ever accorded a ballplayer, living or dead. (This day preceded the Addie Joss benefit by more than a year.) Shibe Park, scene of Doc Powers' abrupt exit from the game he loved, had served to stage a testimony to his character. It gave Philadelphia fans something to be proud of. They had not forgotten.

The Louisville Colonels of 1890

Bob Bailey

The 1991 World Series featured two teams that had finished in the cellar of their division the year before. The Minnesota Twins and the Atlanta Braves became the first teams to go from last to first in a single season...since the first team to do it, in 1890.

It is difficult for baseball writers to think in terms of baseball in the nineteenth century. Sometimes it seems difficult for writers to go back any farther than 1950. It is convenient to think of baseball history beginning with the arrival of the American League in 1901, but baseball was played and records were set before Teddy Roosevelt became President.

In 1889, the Louisville Colonels of the American Association set a season record for losses. In that campaign, they managed to drop 111 contests while winning but 27, for a .196 winning percentage. In comparison, the 1962 Mets had a .250 winning percentage. Louisville was a bad team, an awful team. One year later, at the end of the 1890 season, Louisville had won 61 more games and had become the first team in Major League history to go from last to first in one season.

The club hit bottom on July 2, 1889, when their record stood at 10–52. A local paper reported that Louisville was "an orphan club, without a manager, without money, and with no one to direct it." Club owner Mordecai Davidson had failed to come to agreement with a local syndicate to sell the demoralized club. Reportedly, he had surrendered the franchise to the Association. It is unclear if the Association ever took receipt of the franchise. It appears that the AA instead took the opportunity to act as broker

and effect the sale of the club to a group of Louisville businessmen for an estimated $6500.

The team muddled through, playing .224 ball the rest of the season, making a change or two, and planning for 1890. The field changes included changing field captains. William "Chicken" Wolf dropped the title, and second baseman Dan Shannon took over. Several players were picked up from minor league teams.

On September 16, some big news hit. Guy Hecker, 33-year-old pitcher-first baseman, and, along with Pete Browning, a Louisville star throughout the 1880s, was released. Hecker still hit for a decent average, but his pitching arm was gone. The move signaled the club's decision to rebuild with new, younger players.

Also announced that day was that John Chapman would return to Louisville as manager. Chapman was a veteran who had piloted the original Louisville National League club in 1876-1877. He knew his way around the baseball world, which was vital, because his chief responsibility would be to rebuild the club. The parsimonious days of President Davidson were over, and immediately after the season, the club stockholders subscribed an additional $15,000 to acquire players. Chapman immediately signed Harry Taylor, a catcher-infielder for the Elmira club in the New York State League, who had just hit .377. He was ticketed to be Louisville's first baseman in 1890.

But events were afoot elsewhere in the baseball world that would have a profound effect on Louisville's 1890 club. Things were coming to a head in the dispute between the Brotherhood, an early union of ballplayers, and the National League owners. Although the National League and American Association were co-signatories to the National Agreement, the NL was the dominant part-

Bob Bailey is a former all-star second baseman for the Clark (NJ) Babe Ruth League, and currently a health care executive living in Goshen, KY.

ner and set most of the policy. There was an ongoing dispute between the players and owners over salaries, the reserve clause, termination benefits, and other items which are still at the core of the contentions between players and owners.

In November, 1889, the Brotherhood announced it would operate a new league in 1890. With this announcement the game was afoot. There was a mad scramble of players and franchises. The Players' League began to sign National League and American Association players. The National League tried to block the Players' League, but dipped into Association rosters to fill a few holes. Brooklyn and Cincinnati of the Association joined the NL. One day later the Association lost another team as Kansas City dropped out to join the Western League. By the time the deck was reshuffled seven of the eight Players' League teams were going head-to-head with NL squads in the same cities, and the American Association had only four teams remaining from those that had finished the 1889 season. In response, the Association put a new franchise in Brooklyn, and added teams in Rochester, Syracuse and Toledo. Three eight-team leagues prepared for the 1890 season.

These shifts certainly didn't hurt Louisville's chances for 1890. The removal of Brooklyn (1889 AA champions) and Cincinnati erased two strong squads from the Association. The new franchises would prove to be lesser competition.

While this franchise dance was going on, the Players' League was out searching for players, and it was no respecter of reserve lists. In the AA each team could reserve fourteen players. Not all teams reserved up to the maximum, and when the AA reserve lists were announced 109 names were included. On Opening Day 1890 only about half (fifty-three) would still be with the same team (see Table 1). On the established franchises, only 45 percent of the reserved players remained.

The player movement was particularly devastating to St. Louis and the Athletic club of Philadelphia. St. Louis, which had been runner-up to Brooklyn in 1889, lost seven players to the Players' League. Five left with player-manager Charles Comiskey for Chicago, including Arlie Latham, Tip O'Neill and Silver King. The Athletic club lost six to the PL, including Harry Stovey, Henry Larkin,

Table 1
Effect of player shifts on reserve rosters in the AA, 1889–1890

Team	Reserv.	Retain.	To NL	To PL	To AA	Out of Majors 1890
Louisville	14	7	0	5	0	2
Philadelphia	14	6	0	6	1	1
Columbus	14	9	1	2	2	0
St. Louis	14	6	0	7	1	0
Baltimore	12	3	2	5	2	0
Brooklyn	13	12	0	1	0	0
Cincinnati	14	10	0	0	2	2
Kansas City	14	NA	2	2	1	9
Totals	109	53	5	28	9	14
Percentages	100	49	5	26	8	12

Lou Bierbauer, Lave Cross and Gus Weyhing. The Baltimore franchise retained only three reserved players.

So, of the teams that had finished ahead of Louisville in 1889, the first-, fourth- fifth- and seventh-place teams had left the league, and the second- and third-place clubs were decimated by defections to the Players' League. Only sixth-place Columbus remained relatively unscathed, retaining nine of fourteen players.

The Louisville squad was not untouched by this player movement, losing five reserved players to the new league. But when a team loses 111 games, it's hard to argue that anyone is a key player. None of the five hit as high as .260 or had driven in as many as 50 runs. The big name of the quintet was Pete Browning, who would join Cleveland and lead the Players' League with a .373 batting average. But for Louisville in 1889 he'd hit .256 with 32 RBIs. He was coming off two years in which his drinking and other health problems had limited him to less than 100 games played. The four other defectors produced in their new cities as they had in Louisville.

Unlike most of the other clubs, Louisville didn't look to its major league rivals to improve its roster. Manager Chapman put his years of baseball travel to good use, and began signing minor leaguers. His first pick-up was Taylor, who would hit .306 as Hecker' replacement, second best on the team. In mid-November he signed Herb Goodall, a teammate of Taylor's at Elmira. Goodall was a good hitting pitcher who would contribute eight wins and some good relief work to the 1890 club.

In March, Chapman signed Charlie Hamburg, a local semi-pro player. Hamburg would take Browning's place in left field. While he would only hit .272, his fielding would make a major contribution to the team. He would cut left field errors by one third and make 229 putouts, best on the team and third best in the AA.

Soon afterwards, Louisville signed Tim Shinnick out of New England to play second base for the recently released Dan Shannon.

With the re-signing of shortstop Phil Tomney, outfielders "Chicken" Wolf and William "Farmer" Weaver and former back-up catcher Jack Ryan, the regulars who would produce the turnaround were set.

The pitching staff had local boys Red Ehret and Scott

Table 2
1890 Louisville Regulars

Player	Age	1890 Ave	R	RBI	Age	1889 Ave	R	RBI
Harry Taylor	24	.306	116	N/A	23	Not in Majors		
Tim Shinnick	23	.256	87	N/A	22	Not in Majors		
Phil Tomney	27	.277	72	N/A	26	.213	61	38
Harry Raymond	28	.259	91	N/A	27	.239	58	47
Chicken Wolf	28	.363*	100	N/A	27	.291	72	57
Farmer Weaver	25	.289	101	N/A	24	.291	62	60
Charlie Hamburg	27	.272	93	N/A	26	Not in Majors		
Jack Ryan	22	.217	43	N/A	21	.177	8	2

Player	Age	W-L	ERA		Age	W-L	ERA	
Scott Stratton	21	34-14	2.36*		20	3-13	3.23	
Red Ehret	22	25-14	2.53		21	10-29	4.80	
George Meakim	25	12-7	2.91		24	Not in Majors		
Herb Goodall	20	8-5	3.39		19	Not in Majors		

* Led League

Stratton returning. Ehret, from the Germantown section of Louisville, had been the putative ace of the 1889 staff with a 10-29 record with a 4.80 ERA. Stratton had had an abysmal sophomore season in 1889. He'd posted a 3-13 record but had a good 3.23 ERA. Along with the rookie Goodall, Chapman found another major league novice. The day before the 1890 season was to open, he signed George Meakim out of the Michigan State League. The Brooklyn native would win 12 of his 15 career major league victories in 1890 (see Table 2).

The pieces to the 1890 puzzle were in place. The striking difference between the 1889 and 1890 lineups is the age of the players. The 1889 team had averaged about 30 years old, with such gray beards as catcher Paul Cook (36), second baseman Dan Shannon (34), Hecker (33) and Browning (31). The average age of the 1890 squad was about 25, with no regular over 28.

The season opener against St. Louis was rained out. On April 18 Louisville began the new season with an 11-8 loss to St. Louis and former Colonel Toad Ramsey. This was the only time during the 1890 season that the Kentucky squad would have a losing record. Ehret beat Jack Stivetts the next day to square the Colonels' record, and by the end of April, Louisville was 7-2 and tied for first place with Rochester.

As the team started winning, the local papers stuck a new nickname on the squad. The Colonels became the Cyclones, because in sportswriters' fancies, their fast start resembled a tornado that swept through Louisville in late March.

Louisville's first road trip was a long thirty-game journey that kept them on the road from May 1 to June 2. The team posted what the previous year would have been a spectacular 11-12 record with seven rain-outs, and their combined 17-14 put them in third place behind the Athletics and Rochester. Only Wolf and Shinnick were hitting over .300.

The Cyclones played a game under .500 for most of June and dropped to 27-25, good for fourth place, nine games behind the Athletics.

On June 28, the club began its run to the pennant with a twenty-game homestand. They swept four from the woeful Brooklyns, with Ehret pitching three, then swept the Athletics and Rochester for twelve straight wins.

Four teams were separated by only 5 games, but instead of excitement over the game on the field, the AA was preoccupied with stormclouds gathering on the financial horizon. There were reports of cash problems in Brooklyn and with the Athletic club. The Brooklyn Association squad was the weakest of three teams in the borough and were drawing very poorly—so poorly that they had started shifting home games to the road. Louisville rudely welcomed the wandering Brooklyns with another four game sweep at the park in the west end to take over first place.

The Athletics' problems looked to be mainly on the field. By early August, they had fallen to fourth place, nine games behind the Cyclones. Their pitching had collapsed. Only Sadie McMahon was pitching consistently and he was starting 40 percent of the Athletics' games.

In late August Louisville found itself in first place, seven games in front of St. Louis. Brooklyn was in the cellar, and sinking. With no hope in sight, the Brooklyn owners disbanded and released all their players.

In emergency session the Association awarded the franchise to Baltimore for the rest of the season.

The Athletic club's problems ignited in early September. Third baseman Denny Lyons was suspended for drunkenness and insubordination. Pitchers Mickey Hughes and Eddie Seward were released. The club was left with one pitcher (McMahon) and used amateurs to fill out its rotation. Reports began to come out of Philadelphia that the club had not paid salaries since July. The club was rumored to be close to disbanding.

Through August, Louisville played at a 15–4 clip and was 6-1/2 games ahead of St. Louis. The Cyclones went 17–8 in September and were in full control of the race. On October 6, Scott Stratton recorded his 33rd win of the season as he beat Columbus 2-0 and Louisville clinched the pennant.

Louisville finished the season with an 88-44 record, ten games ahead of Columbus. A 61-game improvement in the win column. From 66-1/2 games behind to pennant winner.

How does a team do that? How does it go from last to first? The accompanying Table 3 compares the team's statistical performances in 1889 and 1890.

The Cyclones scored 187 more runs in 1890 than 1889. That's a 28 percent increase, while the league scoring as a whole suffered an 11 percent decrease. They led the league in batting with a .279 average. They were second in slugging and stolen bases. In most other batting categories Louisville was in the middle of the pack. Improvement for sure, but not 61 games worth.

The big story is the opposition runs. After giving up a league leading 1091 runs in 1889 (up to that point only Association teams in New York and Cleveland in 1887 had yielded more) they dropped 46 percent to 588. The total

| Category | LOUISVILLE | | | A A | | |
	1890	1889	Percent Change	1890	1889	Percent Change
Wins	88*	27†	226			
Losses	44*	111†	-60			
Runs	819	632†	28	6042	6783	-11
Opp Runs	588	1091†	-46	6042	6783	-11
2B	156	170	-8	1258	1493	-16
3B	65	75	-13	559	619	-10
HR	15	22	-32	188	296	-36
BA	.279*	.252†	11	.253	.262	-3
SA	.350	.330	6	.332	.354	-6
SB	341	203†	68	2612	2729	-4
E	380*	584	-35	3459	3992	-13
DP	79	117	-32	739	855	-14
FA	.933*	.907	3	.923	.916	1
CG	114	127	-10	962	982	-2
BB	293*	475	-38	3747	3704	1
SO	587	451	30	4233	4177	1
SHO	13	2	650	49	50	-2
ERA	2.58*	4.81†	-46	3.86	3.84	1

Table 3
Louisville vs. American Association, 1889-1890

*Best in league
†Worst in league

swing on runs scored and opposition runs was 690.

How do you make the opposition score half the runs against you that they did the year before? There are only two ways: pitching and defense. And Louisville had them both.

The pitching staff had an amazing turnaround. From last to first in wins, ERA and runs yielded. The ERA dropped 2.23 runs per game. Walks dropped almost 40 percent. Shutouts went from two to thirteen.

Stratton and Ehret had dream seasons. Stratton in particular had a career year and then some. He was 34-14 with a 2.36 ERA. He led the league in ERA, winning percentage and fewest walks. Red Ehret was 25-14, and was second in the Association with a 2.53 ERA. Stratton and Ehret would each have only one other winning season.

But you don't improve 60-plus games on pitching alone. As impressive as the pitching was, the fielding was even better.

In 1889 the team had the most errors and second-worst fielding percentage in the AA. In 1890 they had the least and the best. They committed 204 fewer errors—an improvement of 1.4 errors per game.

Offensively, only Chicken Wolf and perhaps Harry Taylor can be said to have had big offensive years. Wolf hit 73 points over his career batting average and won the batting title (see Table 4). But everyone except Harry Raymond, Farmer Weaver and Jack Ryan can be said to have had career years—in very undistinguished careers. Phil Tomney, Charlie Hamburg and Herb Goodall never again appeared in the majors. Taylor, Tim Shinnick and George Meakim had careers of four years or less. Taylor, Shinnick, Meakim and Goodall were rookies.

For the rest of the franchise's life—mostly against tougher, more stable competition—it would finish seventh once, eighth once, ninth three times, eleventh once and twelfth three times. By 1892, only two players—Weaver and Stratton—would remain with the squad.

But the Louisville Cyclones of 1890 had their moment in the sun. The factors of new ownership, huge turnover in Association rosters due to the Brotherhood War and a group of players performing as a team as they never would again, brought Louisville its only major league pennant. And, with due respect to Minnesota and Atlanta, the first major league team to go from last to first.

Table 4
Louisville Regulars

1889

	Age	BA	HR	RBI	OP	A	E	FA
1B Guy Hecker	33	.284	1	36	609	23	20	.969
2B Dan Shannon	34	.257	4	48	307	391	69	.910
SS Phil Tomney	26	.213	4	38	229	454	114	.857
3B Harry Raymond	27	.239	0	47	206	261	60	.886
RF Chicken Wolf	27	.291	3	57	159	16	10	.946
CF Farmer Weaver	24	.291	0	60	249	30	25	.918
LF Pete Browning	31	.256	2	32	152	12	22	.882
C Paul Cook	36	.227	0	15	293	138*	35	.925

1890

	Age	BA	HR	RBI	OP	A	E	FA
1B Harry Taylor	24	.306	0	NA	1301	51	25	.982
2B Tim Shinnick	23	.256	1	NA	288	351	52	.925
SS Phil Tomney	27	.277	1	NA	180	406	64	.902
3B Harry Raymond	28	.259	2	NA	182	241	61	.874
RF Chicken Wolf	28	.363*	4	NA	199	16	14	.939
CF Farmer Weaver	25	.289	3	NA	227	23	18	.933
LF Chas. Hamburg	27	.272	3	NA	229	16	14	.946
C Jack Ryan	22	.217	0	NA	415	148	41*	.932

*Led League

One win, the strange way

When 83-year-old Tom Glass died in 1981, his obituary in the Greensboro (NC) Record *proudly proclaimed that he had played briefly for the old Philadelphia Athletics, winning one game and losing none. Glass gained that victory in an unusual manner on June 15, 1925, when he pitched three innings of relief as the A's were getting trounced 15–4 going into the bottom of the eighth. With the game seemingly out of hand, Glass batted and flied out. However, eight batters later there was still just one out and Glass sat down for a pinch hitter as the A's tallied 13 runs in one of the greatest comebacks in major league history to win 17–15, generating that one victory for Glass.*

Loaded with talent...and that doesn't even count the manager!

Seven future members of the Hall of Fame were in the Philadelphia A's lineup at the same time in the ninth inning of the club's June 11, 1927 game. The A's outfield consisted of Ty Cobb in right, Al Simmons in center, and Zack Wheat in left. Jimmie Foxx was at first base, Eddie Collins at second base, and Lefty Grove was pitching in relief. Cy Perkins had started behind the plate, but in the ninth, Mickey Cochrane pinch hit for him seventh in the batting order. For a brief few moments before number nine batter Grove was pulled for a pinch hitter, seven future Hall-of-Famers were representing Connie Mack's club.

—Charlie Bevis

The 1930 Phillies

John Thom

Okay, baseball fans, put your trivia hats on, it's Quiz Time! Can you identify the following players?

We'll call out their names slowly, and as soon as you know who they are, stop us. Ready? Here we go. John Milligan...Buz Phillips...Harry Smythe...Chet Nichols. No? Want a hint? They're National Leaguers. Here's more. Byron Speece...Hal Elliott...Lou Koupal. Another hint? Sure. Same team. Ready again? Snipe Hansen...Hap Collard...Pete Alexander. Now do you know? You don't? Well, okay, one more hint. It's a pitching staff. We're practically giving it away. All right, more names. Ray Benge...Les Sweetland...Phil Collins...Claude Willoughby.

Wait! There's a hand in the back. Yes? What? Louder, please. The 1930 Philadelphia Phillies pitching staff? Give the fan a cigar, we've got a winner! Which name gave it away? We named them all. Willoughby? Not surprising. He probably epitomizes the 1930 Phillies more than anyone else.

You'll remember this team as the outfit that batted .315 for the year, scored 944 runs...and *still* finished dead last in the league, 40 games behind the leader. It was said of the Phillies of this era that on a clear day they could see seventh place. The question is, if they could hit so well, why couldn't they win? The answer is the list of names we just read. The Phillies lacked in pitching what they had an abundance of in hitting—talent.

We're going to look back at these pitchers and see why they have been branded as one of the worst staffs in big league history. At one point during the season someone

John Thom is a business communications specialist. He lives in Los Angeles.

NBL

Les Sweetland. 7–11, 7.71.

wrote, "The Phillies have frequently finished last, but they never have had a worse looking tail-ender than the 1930 ensemble...It's the old trouble with a daily example of slovenly pitching to nullify the batting power of the team, but flinging is as much a part of baseball as anything else and a team not equipped with pitching strength never can hope to get anywhere no matter how they boast about their batters."

And boast they could. Chuck Klein hit .386, rapped 40 home runs, set a record with 59 doubles, and drove home 170 runs. In home games alone, Klein hit .439 with 26 homers and 109 RBI. By contrast, Claude Willoughby won four games and lost 17, giving up more than 14 hits per nine innings, more than 8-1/2 runs per game, and finishing with an earned run average of 7.59.

Defending NL batting champion Lefty O'Doul hit .383. On the other hand, Les Sweetland was 7–15 and had an ERA of 7.71, the highest ever recorded by a pitcher in 154 innings or more. Though they appeared in fewer innings, five other pitchers on the staff had ERAs higher even than Sweetland's.

Pinky Whitney hit .342, Don Hurst batted .327 and Bernie Friberg hit .341. Then there were the pitchers, two of whom collected 27 of the team's 52 victories, while the remaining twelve combined for 25 wins...and lost 76!

The ace of the staff was Fidgety Phil Collins, who went 16–11 with an ERA of 4.78. One scribe of the day named Collins as his outstanding National League pitcher for 1930 for doing so well with such a futile team. In fact, the name usually appended to the "Quakers" was the "Phutile Phillies." How futile? Twenty-one times the team scored eight runs or more and still lost. On nine occasions, the Phils scored in double figures and still couldn't win. In July, they were beaten 16–15 and 19–15 in back-to-back games. Nine different Phils pitchers plodded to the mound in the two games.

It was, to say the least, a generous pitching staff. Joe Vila of the *New York Sun* said the Phillies were "equipped with the weakest lot of pitchers seen in the National League in many years."

Of course, they were aided in this generosity by a defense that led both leagues in errors. The team's 239 errors translates to more than one and a half per game. As a consequence, the runs allowed averages of the pitchers are dramatically higher than their ERAs. Only two of the 14 pitchers allowed fewer than seven runs per nine innings pitched. You'll recall that the team set a record that may never be broken when it allowed opponents 1,199 runs over the year. That's 7.7 runs per game. To win even 52 games the Phillies needed an offense that could hit .315!

Why was Burt Shotton, the Phils' manager, saddled with this bunch of pitching misfits? The answer is cloaked in the mists of time. But a possible explanation lies in the reputation that William Baker had for not pursuing or retaining top-flight players. The Phillies' owner was, to be courteous, a careful spender. To illustrate, the story went around in 1929 that he put a screen atop the short right field wall in Baker Bowl to prevent Chuck Klein, who was on his way to a National League home run record, from hitting too many homers. Baker feared that Klein, in the mold of Babe Ruth, would have high salary demands over the winter. The Phils' owner explained that the screen was intended to dampen "cheap" home runs.

Baker was also accused of trading away talented players, undoubtedly to keep a lid on salary expenses. After the June trading deadline in 1930, Joe Williams, sports editor of the *New York Telegram*, reported, "The pressure in the last 24 hours of the trading period was especially strong on William Baker, owner of the Phillies, who used to have a price on anything within his dilapidated ball yard. His club is destined to finish somewhere in the second division. The financial outlook for the second half of the campaign is not so bright. Yet Baker held on to Benge, Thompson, Thevenow, Whitney and Sothern, waiving away a sizable amount. Perhaps he finally has caught the spirit of the patient Burton Shotton, a really capable manager trying to get somewhere." Baked died in December 1930, just weeks after trading O'Doul and Thompson, two of the team's stars.

Admittedly, the Phillies were only one of sixteen big league teams seeking more pitching in this era of the live ball. Every team, with the possible exception of the Philadelphia A's, could lament a lack of pitching. Hitters had free rein. Collectively, the National League batted .303, and was a couple of hits away from making it .304.

Doormats for many years in the league, the Phils surprised everyone in 1929 by rising from the cellar to fifth place, based mostly on a surge over the last two months of the season. Big things were expected from them in 1930, and 43-year-old Pete Alexander was counted on for some of it. Alex was a 373-game winner and a legendary figure by the time 1930 rolled around. When he was acquired over the winter, the Phils saw him as a source of strength and potentially enough wins to put them into contention in 1930. Unfortunately, Alex went 0–3 before getting his release early in June. It was a sad end to a great career. He was completely ineffective. In nine appearances he was scored on each time.

The rest of the Philadelphia staff not only lacked the Hall of Fame credentials of a Grover Cleveland Alexander, but also most of them lacked minimum big league qualifications. Phil Collins, who won 16 games, and Ray Benge, who won 11, represented the only pitchers on the staff who still had any notable big league productivity left in their arms. Three others who had anything like a big league career to look back upon—the great Pete Alexander, Les Sweetland and Claude Willoughby—were washed up. The other nine pitchers were untested. And when they took their major league exams in 1930, they scored Ds and Fs. The National League that year was not the place for an unskilled pitcher to try his hand at the profession.

Benge was in his third year with the team and had limited success in the early going. But there were other times in the campaign when Ray may have doubted his own abilities. In July, he started seven games, pitching 43-$^2/_3$ innings. He lost five of the starts as part of a personal seven-game losing streak, allowing 72 hits, 54 runs (11.1 per nine innings), and 42 earned runs (8.6 ERA). On July 17 against Cincinnati, Benge allowed 16 hits and 14 runs (nine earned) in eight innings as he was beaten 14–9. In his next start six days later against Pittsburgh, Ray was pounded for six hits and six runs in two-plus innings as the Phils absorbed a 16–15 loss. Both games were played at Baker Bowl.

Byron Speece had been up for two cups of coffee in the American League in the mid-'20s, then got a shot with the '30 Phils. In 20 innings, he allowed 29 earned runs. Opposing batters hit .432 against him. Speece appeared in 11 games from April 23 to July 10 and the Phils' opponents scored in double figures all 11 times. On June 23 at Wrigley Field in Chicago, Speece gave the Cubs 11 runs in 3-$^2/_3$ innings. On July 10 in only one-third of an inning, he allowed seven runs on seven hits to the New York Giants. It was his last game in the majors.

Buz Phillips saw his only major league action in August and September of 1930. He pitched only 44 innings and had an ERA of 7.98. In his fourth pitching assignment, on August 18 at Chicago, Buz relieved Snipe Hansen and in 5-$^1/_3$ innings turned a problem into a disaster. He was treated roughly by the Cubs, who scored 12 runs on 12 hits and five walks, defeating Philadelphia, 17–3. The Cubs repeated the salvo against him at Baker Bowl on September 12. Phillips relieved Willoughby this time, and in six innings he yielded 13 hits and two walks, which accounted for 11 runs. Chicago beat Philadelphia, 17–4.

Roy "Snipe" Hansen was purchased in mid-summer from the Class B Central League "for the highest amount ever paid for a player from the league." In three months he lost seven games, failing to win any. His ERA was 6.75. You might argue that Roy lived with bad luck. In his first three games, he was dunned for 15 runs, but only six were earned. Likewise, one of his losses was a 2–1 complete game setback to Pittsburgh. In the two games just prior, the Phils had scored 18 runs; in the two games following, they scored 30. In four more seasons in the 1930s, Hansen managed to win 22 games.

Lou Koupal joined the Phils in 1929 from Brooklyn. After going 0–4 in three months in 1930, he was sold to Baltimore in the International League. He resurfaced in 1937 with the St. Louis Browns. In 37 innings with the Phils in 1930, he allowed 35 runs, all earned. Lou appeared in 13 games for Philadelphia in 1930 and the Quakers lost all 13. Koupal was one out from a complete game victory on April 19, the Phils' second game of the year, when he allowed the Giants to snatch a 3–2 win with two runs in the ninth inning. It was downhill from there.

Downhill aptly describes Hap Collard, who had seen momentary service with the Cleveland Indians in '27 and '28. His only other big league experience was in 1930 and it looked when he got underway with the Phils that they had a winner in the righthander. His first five appearances were in relief and he displayed real effectiveness, winning two games and losing one, that on a lone run. Shotton moved Collard to a starting spot and Hap responded with two complete game wins over pennant contenders Brooklyn and St. Louis. At four wins and a loss, this guy looked like a lifesaver. But the bubble burst in mid-June, and thereafter he went 2–11 with an ERA of 8.60. It also spelled the end of his major league career.

The end may have been hastened on August 17 in the eighth inning of a game against Chicago when Collard gave up two walks, hit a batter and then allowed a single, which contributed to two runs and another lost game. Collard was relieved, and after the inning ended he and Tony Rensa, his catcher, got into an argument. Rensa said Collard crossed him up by not throwing the pitches called for. Words led to punches between the two before they were separated. In eight more appearances in 1930 after the tete-a-tete with Rensa, Collard was handled roughly each time by opposing teams.

Harry Smythe was in his second year. He was 4–6 with the Phils in '29, but failed to win a game in '30, losing three. His welcome ran out at the end of August when Shotton turned to others on the staff. He returned to the majors in 1934, splitting time between the Yankees and the Dodgers. He was 1–3 that year. In 1930, Harry was a harbinger of high-scoring games. In his 25 appearances, the opposition scored eight runs or more 22 times off Phillies pitching, and 16 times they hit double figures.

John Milligan was a puzzle. He had seen spare duty with the Phils in 1928 and 1929. He started the 1930 season with the team, but he was shipped out in May only to be recalled in September. Though he appeared in only 28 innings, his ERA of 3.21 was respectable. He also allowed batters a small .255 batting average, but when he yielded nearly seven walks per nine innings, the scales tipped against him. He saw even less duty with the Phils in 1931, and then in 1934 with the Senators.

For some reason, Chet Nichols, who had pitched briefly for the Pirates and Giants from 1926 to 1928, was a spring holdout with the Phils in 1930. Now this was a good year for holdouts, but Nichols was not in the same class as some who put the squeeze on their employers. Babe Ruth, for example, got $80,000 a year for two seasons. Al Simmons, the A's great outfielder, signed just before the first pitch of the season, then hit a home run his first time up. Edd Roush pulled the ultimate holdout, not signing with the Giants all year!

Nichols, however, held out and, after signing, was ineligible until June. He then proceeded to win one game. It was his only major league victory in six seasons. In 60 innings in 1930, he allowed 51 runs, 45 earned, for an

Claude Willoughby, the hitters' friend—to the tune of .369.

ERA of 6.75. A holdout!

Hal Elliott was Johnny-on-the-spot for the Phils in 1930, his second year with the team. He appeared in a league-leading 48 games, including 11 starts. But he embodied the generosity of the staff when he allowed opposing hitters a .382 batting average. His ERA was 7.69. He gave up 120 runs in 117 innings. His six wins was fourth best on the staff. He lost 11.

The giant of the staff was Collins. He won 16 and lost only 11. He led the team in complete games with 17 and innings with 239. His ERA of 4.78 was no great shakes, but in the context of the "Year of the Hitter," it was not so bad either. Bill Dooly of the *Philadelphia Record* noted, "The Phillies had a one-man pitching staff this year. Its name was Phil Collins. His record is sufficient to stamp him, with the writer, as the best pitcher in the National League." Collins had several more productive years with the Phils, finishing his career with 80 wins.

The last two pitchers on the team were perhaps the most inglorious of the lot. Les Sweetland, he of the 7.71 ERA, and Claude Willoughby, 4–17 on the year with a 7.59 ERA, probably contributed the most to rounding out the story of the history-making 1930 Phillies staff.

Sweetland even laid the groundwork for unwarranted optimism when he was tabbed as opening day pitcher and proceeded to shut out the Brooklyn Robins, 1–0, on a lovely three-hitter. James Isaminger of the *Philadelphia Inquirer* said Sweetland's work "was an epic, and belied the current spring fiction that Burt Shotton has no dependable pitchers." Tommy Holmes of the *Brooklyn Eagle* noted how Sweetland was "pitching with easy nonchalance and confidence."

Could it be that the Phillies were going to get some good pitching to go along with their stunning batting attack? Well, they didn't. Sweetland was treated badly by the league all year, giving up more than 14.5 hits per game. Opposing batters hit .373 against the lefthander. After a turn with the Cubs in 1931, Sweetland was out of the majors.

And Willoughby? He, too, threw a shutout in '30, but outside of that and a couple of other commendable games, he was a punching bag for the league's hitters. His opponents' batting average was .369, and with four walks per game, his opponents' on base percentage was a lofty .418. In 1931 he was 0–2 with the Pirates and then gone from the majors.

Years later, the Phils second baseman of the time, Fresco Thompson, recalled the pitchers and said they were "really awful." He took the lineup card up to home plate before one game, as was his custom as team captain, and in the ninth spot, the one commonly reserved for the starting pitcher, he had written, "Willoughby—and others," a timeless tribute to the 1930 Philadelphia Phillies.

Phils pitchers made 357 appearances on the mound in 1930. Their generosity was most abundant. Phils pitchers gave up ten runs or more in 45 games. They allowed 15 runs or more 17 times and more than 20 runs three times. Starting pitchers were scored on in every outing except for the three shutouts by Sweetland, Collins and Willoughby. Relief pitchers were scored on in 142 of 201 appearances, or 71 percent of the time. And these were not just the runners they inherited, these were runs charged to their own pitching.

In only six games did pitchers appear in a game and go beyond three innings of work without allowing a run, and that includes the three shutouts. In the 357 mound appearances, Phils pitchers were scored on 285 times, or 80 percent of the time.

In late July, the Phils lost 11 games in a row. The first loss was a 2–1 heartbreaker to Pittsburgh. The next ten defy description. Philadelphia allowed 113 runs: 16, 19, 9, 16, 10, 9, 5, 11, 9, 9. The Phils' offense scored 67 runs in the ten games and still couldn't win one.

The Phils were not scheduled on September 3, 4 or 5 in

1930. At home on Friday, September 2, Philadelphia was blasted by the Giants, 18–5. Four Phillies pitchers absorbed the beating. On September 6, the Phils were at Ebbets Field to face Brooklyn. As if to help them redeem themselves, Burt Shotton sent the same four pitchers to the mound. Three days of leisure and wound-licking had not helped. The Phils were bombed, 22–8. Collard, Elliott, Phillips and Sweetland allowed 40 runs in back-to-back games.

This is not a pretty picture. It took fortitude to watch these men at work. Isaminger wrote, "Some of the scores (at home) have been positively fantastical, and certainly not suggestive of baseball at its best."

Gentlemen and sensitive ladies in the City of Brotherly Love often had to turn away and not look as the Phillies pitchers went about their labors. But all too often their gaze was drawn suddenly back to the field as a ball rattled noisily off the tin wall in right field at cozy Baker Bowl.

Indeed, the wall in right field was uncomfortably close for members of the pitching fraternity, just 280 feet down the line and about 300 in the "power" alley. Power alley? With the live ball in use at the time and the free-swinging of the hitters, it didn't take much to drive a ball to the fences in some National League ball yards. Baker Bowl—referred to once as a "Ford-sized" park—led the pack with its easy target in right.

It's no secret that many opposing pitchers found reasons to be unavailable for mound duty when their teams came into Philadelphia. Brooklyn lefthander Jumbo Jim Elliott raged at Baker Bowl one day, exclaiming, "Look back over your scorebook. You'll find that three-quarters of the Philadelphia hits were slapped up against that high wall and were fly balls that would have been outs in a decent ball park. It sounds nice to say that what's fair for one team is fair for the other, but it isn't true. The Phillies play 77 games a season here. They know their stuff. They get so much practice bouncing them off the right field fence that they become perfect. They'd probably win the pennant if they could play all their games at home."

Two notes should be made here. One, the Phillies of that era couldn't have won a pennant if they played all their games in Heaven and had God on their side—the Phils' home record in 1930 was just 35–42. And two, Elliott was traded to the Phillies after the close of the 1930 season and won a league-high 19 games for them in 1931. Go figure!

How close was that right field wall at Baker Bowl? It was so convenient to the infield that right fielder Chuck Klein set a major league record in 1930 with 44 assists, 33 of them at home in the shadow of the tin wall.

So you can't put all the blame on the pitchers for the team's record. They carried on half of their labors in a park suited for hitting. Perhaps the best thing that can be said for them is that they were lucky they didn't have to pitch to Klein, O'Doul and the rest of the Phillies hitters. But then, it was bad luck for Klein, O'Doul and the other Phillies hitters that they didn't have the chance to face their own hurlers.

At one point during the season, even Burt Shotton tried to divert blame away from the Phillies pitchers. After Philadelphia ended an 11-game losing streak, Shotton said he felt that part of the bad showing of the team had been due to "the razzing of spectators at the local park."

Maybe it was one of those frustrated spectators who sneaked into Baker Bowl one night and went to the familiar and prominent advertisement on the right field wall that read, "The Phillies Use Lifebuoy Soap." On it, he added the words, "And they still stink."

Déja vu all over again

No clan of men on the face of the globe earn their money easier than the professional base ball players, as they only work two hours a day when they work at all, and their salaries vary from fifty to one hundred and fifty dollars a week. Still they are constantly complaining of being overworked and they have to be coaxed and humored like a lot of spoiled children. Why, were it nor for base ball the majority of these whiners and complainers would not be able to make a living, as they are too infernally lazy to make a success even at carrying the hod. If the managers only had the backbone to lay every one of these lazy whelps off without pay and fill their places with younger blood, or crowd them out of the business altogether, it will work a radical change and give the public base ball exhibitions well worth seeing. —From The National Police Gazette, *October 16, 1886.*

—Jack Kavanagh

The Continental League of 1921

David Pietrusza

Baseball had it rough during the teens. After beating back the Federal League's serious challenge in 1914 and 1915, it faced and survived—although just barely—the challenge of the World War. In fact, the 1918 season was shortened, ending at Labor Day, and baseball had to receive a special dispensation from the federal government before it could play the World Series. Only the collapse of Imperial Germany saved baseball for the 1919 season.

The game then emerged into the lively ball era of Babe Ruth, with increased hitting and attendance, and as it did it was met with yet another of the short-lived, farcical rivals that had marked the early 1910s. This time the "challenge" emanated from Boston in the form of the "Continental League."

Championing it was George Herman "Andy" Lawson, whom *The Sporting News* characterized as "famous as [a] baseball promoter in the past." Announcements Lawson distributed described him—albeit in somewhat confusing terms—as "the father of the old United States League, which later developed into the Federal League." Others recalled him as the organizer of another recent flop called the "Greater Boston League."

Assisting him in this new endeavor were James Nelson Barry and George Maynard Riley, also of Beantown. Barry, whose residence was given as 433 Shawmut Avenue, was moderately known as a promoter of New England area semi-pro teams. He had also been a sort of talent scout or "bird dog" for big league clubs. Riley, of 15 Park Square, was totally unknown in baseball circles.

David Pietrusza, author of Major Leagues *and* Baseball's Canadian-American League *was Associate Editor of* Total Baseball *(Third Edition). His* Lights On!: The Story of Night Baseball *will be published by A&M this year.*

The Sporting News termed Lawson an "Old Friend" and seemed to be taking the announcement at least semi-seriously, reporting the circuit would be a "big league" and "a real rival of the American and the National," although details of how it would obtain its players were not discussed.

On December 28, 1920, the Continental League was chartered under the laws of the State of Massachusetts, capitalized at $60,000. Lawson held 4,000 shares of its common stock; Barry held 3,000, and Riley owned 2,000. The following day an organizational meeting was held.

On December 31, Lawson announced that his league would represent not cities, as had been the traditional arrangement, but states (shades of the Minnesota Twins, Texas Rangers and California Angels). The Massachusetts club would operate in Boston; New York State's in either Brooklyn or Buffalo; New Jersey's in Camden; Pennsylvania's in Pittsburgh; Maryland's in Baltimore; Michigan's in Detroit; Ohio's in Cleveland; and Indiana's in Indianapolis. In no case would there be more than one team per state.

Offices of the new circuit would be at 27 School Street, opposite the Boston City Hall.

Major League baseball was prosperous, and in any case, was not about to be cowed by a circuit capitalized at a mere $60,000 (although there was talk of the Maryland franchise being backed by $2,000,000).

"Let 'em come along into Brooklyn," challenged the Robins' Secretary Charles H. Ebbets, Jr., "if they have two or three million dollars to invest in grounds and a plant they will have everything they need except ball players—and, of course, that is only a minor item in getting a team of major leaguers together.

"I don't think there is much to get excited over in this proposition. Evidently somebody up Boston was having a Happy New Year."

Ebbets heaped further ridicule on the Continental League's choices of Camden ("When [it] is included as one of the cities in the new league there is no hesitation in regarding the circuit as something of a joke") and Indianapolis, which he recalled as a city that won a Federal League pennant and then saw its team move to Newark.

"It is difficult," concluded Ebbets, "to consider a major league without teams in New York, Philadelphia, Chicago or St. Louis, but they do try some odd things in baseball now and then."

The *New York Times* took care to point out further difficulties Lawson and company would be facing. The courts had recently given grudging backing to the standard player contract. Parks were now more expensive. After the Feds' failure, men of wealth would be

Charles Ebbets, right, at about the time he was underwhelmed by the Continental League, with Cincinnati manager Pat Moran, left, and his own skipper, Wilbert Robinson.

less inclined to back a third league. "It is not likely," the *Times* reasoned, "that major league club owners will view the proposed organization with any great alarm...."

However, restiveness was in the air within Organized Baseball's ranks. The International League and the American Association were grumbling about breaking away from the National Association. Controversy centered over the draft prices paid by big league clubs for minor league players.

"The Indianapolis club," said Indians manager Jack Hendricks, "is solidly back of any move that President [Thomas Jefferson] Hickey may take to lead the American Association from the smaller loops into a larger one."

Nonetheless, Lawson seemed to make no moves to take advantage of this discontent.

On January 4, 1921, "Andy" Lawson was officially named President of the mysterious new circuit. Along with this news came another of what would soon be a whole series of conflicting news releases concerning prospective franchises. Now missing was any mention of a Pennsylvania franchise. In its place was the possibility of one for "the Province of Ontario, with a team at Toronto."

Lawson was off and rolling in any case. There would be no salary limits on Continental League clubs, and Lawson extended a fantastic offer to financially hard-pressed Red Sox owner Harry H. Frazee to purchase Fenway Park. He added nonchalantly: "In the event of the Red Sox not accepting the offer to sell, a park will be built in Boston."

Other names now emerged. Fred Lundy was awarded the Boston franchise, although it was said he was a mere agent for others. The Indiana slot was given over to Indianapolis' Donald Jones; the New Jersey franchise to Philadelphia's Charles H. Mack.

On January 9, The *New York Times* reported that Lawson was surveying the New York metropolitan area for possible playing sites. Old Federal League locations at Newark (Harrison Field) and Brooklyn (Washington Park) were examined, although Lawson indicated that either city might be replaced as its state's prospective representative—Newark by Camden; Brooklyn by far-off Buffalo. In fact, the possibility of any Garden State club now seemed iffy.

In terms of player personnel Lawson indicated that the Continental League (which the *Times* alternately termed the "Continental Baseball Association") had already signed several "prominent" players, as well as some umpires, although Andy would not reveal their identities. Players would be engaged for one season only—there would be no reserve clause. Despite rumors to the contrary, players involved in the recent Black Sox scandal were not being considered.

The *Times* was intrigued and amused by another of Lawson's ideas, that he would be engaging "negro or Cuban" talent, primarily for his Massachusetts, Pennsylvania and New Jersey squads. The paper noted that such a move would "insure him the 135th Street and Lenox Avenue [Harlem] vote quite solidly." Lawson himself commented that both Philadelphia and Boston contained large black populations, hinting that these could be a significant percentage of his gate. "He asserted," reported the *Times*, "that there were at least 100 ball players in this country who were the equal in playing skill of the average sound player in the two major leagues..." It was not a popular opinion for the time, but it was, of course, true.

Regarding franchises, Lawson claimed that three of the eight possible clubs had already been assigned, the aforementioned Indianapolis and Boston teams, plus Toronto. Lawson piously hoped to have as many players from the state or province that each club represented as possible. He also hoped to buy existing clubs and/or stadiums if they were available.

Capital for the new circuit, Lawson maintained, was now at the $75,000 level.

Lawson's next stop was Philadelphia. From the City of Brotherly Love, he announced that the Continental League's season would commence on May 1 and end just after Labor Day. Franchises would now be awarded to: Massachusetts (Boston); Indiana (Indianapolis); New York (Brooklyn); New Jersey (Newark); Pennsylvania (either Philadelphia or Pittsburgh); Maryland (Baltimore); Ohio (Cleveland); and either Ontario (Toronto) or Michigan (Detroit).

Aside from the daily shifting of franchises, other statements by Lawson were guaranteed to raise eyebrows. Each CL club would be affiliated with the American Federation of Labor and, of course, there would be no reserve clause, "as the Continental does not recognize such contracts."

Lawson continued his campaign to obtain the former Federal League stadia, firing off a telegram to Cincinnati Reds President Garry Herrmann (the former National Commission Chairman), ordering him to "cut the strings" on the Newark and Brooklyn fields. "Otherwise," the promoter threatened, "I shall immediately sign four American League players who wish to jump to the Continental League."

Still in Philadelphia a few days later, Lawson contradicted himself once more. Now, he stated that he would indeed sign the disgraced (but still not judged in a court of law) Black Sox players.

Other announcements were to come, but were not calculated to inspire the baseball public. Minor League catcher Harry O'Donnell (an Athletics property) was dickering with the Continentals—amazingly, it was said he could virtually name his price. Former Red Sox and Buffed infielder Clyde "Hack" Engle was set to become pilot of the CL Boston team. Darby, Pennsylvania resident Eddie Bohon was attempting to secure the Camden franchise.

More interesting was Lawson's flirtation with black talent. The Chicago American Giants were mentioned as a prospective franchise, although that club was already a member of Rube Foster's new National Association of Colored Professional Base Ball Clubs. Two other black teams, the obscure Boston Tigers and the Knoxville Giants, were also mentioned as possible CL members.

By early February two more franchises were formally awarded: to shoe manufacturer Warren L. Patterson in Buffalo (this meant Brooklyn was out of the running) and to Captain Raymond C. Warner in Philadelphia (this spelled *finis* for Pittsburgh).

Shortly thereafter, Lawson was on the move again, heading for Pittsburgh, Cleveland and either Cincinnati or Chicago to line up backers. Again he was hinting at black participation, boasting that four Negro clubs were knocking on his door.

As Opening Day approached less and less was heard of Andy Lawson and his Continental League. By late April, he popped up announcing that play would not begin on May 1, but would instead start on May 20.

It never did.

The Milkman

Dutch Doyle

The Roaring Twenties and the Dreary Depression produced exciting sandlot baseball all over the country. Philadelphia was no exception. Here, in the early twenties, the best teams modeled their organizations on the Major Leagues. The players signed contracts and—at least through 1924 or so—were paid twice a month.

Some of the great teams in the Philadelphia area were organized by the department stores like Lit Brothers and Strawbridge & Clothier. Some were formed by Catholic Churches: Ascension, Nativity and St. Anne's. Others simply represented different neighborhoods: Kensington, Nicetown, Wentz Olney, South Phillies, North Phillies, and Port Richmond.

Real old timers who lived through this golden age of sandlot ball remember many legendary feats and players. The legend that looms largest is the one and only Rube Chambers, who was known as the Milkman because he serviced a regular route for a local dairy. Rube could pitch, hit, and handle first base with the best. He played every night of the week, and for the right price he would *pitch* every night of the week. In those days, sore arms seem to have been alien to pitchers! They hadn't heard about lifting weights, so they threw every day. After pitching a game, they rubbed their own arms with a fifteen cent bottle of wintergreen.

The Milkman was one of these rubber arm guys who could throw into eternity, and in September of 1932 he was involved in a most intriguing weekend. He played for

many teams, but one of his main organizations in 1932 was the Frankford Legion, who played their games at Baldwin Field at Large and Pratt Streets in Philadelphia.

The manager of the Legion was Harry Lowe, who was a good friend of Kensington's Jimmy Wilson, the catcher for the World Champion St. Louis Cardinals. Harry wanted to honor Jimmy, and somehow he arranged for the Cards to play the Legion on Tuesday night, September 6, under portable lights. This was history for the Frankford neighborhood.

Now, the Cardinals intended to give the fans a real treat. They show-cased their newest sensation, Ducky Medwick, in center field. Ducky was flanked by Rip Collins in right and George Puccinelli, who later played regularly for the 1936 A's, in left. The infield had Sunny Jim Bottomley, Jimmy Reese (alias James Herman Solomon), Jake Flowers and Pepper Martin. Allyn Stout and Sylvester Johnson shared mound duty, with Jimmy Wilson and Gus Mancuso behind the plate. Coach Buzzy Wares was used as a pinch hitter.

The Legion had a veteran team with much experience and savvy. Dick Spalding and Denny Sothern were former big league players. Eddie Roetz, an excellent shortstop, had been up with the St. Louis Browns for sixteen games in 1929. His was a unique career as in those sixteen games he played all four infield positions. Hard hitting Howard Lohr, forty years of age, patrolled left field. Howard had been up with the Reds in 1914. The crowd-pleasing Lefty Holstein, a local legend in his own right, held first base, and to his right was smooth fielding, hard hitting Honey Muffler. Fred Sharkey handled the pitches of Philadelphia's greatest sandlot phenomenon, Rube "The Milkman" Chambers.

Ed "Dutch" Doyle is a retired teacher in Philadelphia.

The game was set for a Tuesday. Any normal human being would have rested on Sunday and Monday so that he could be 100 percent on Tuesday night for the World Champs. To Rube, though, Tuesday was too far away to even think about. Besides, there was money to be made on Sunday and Monday. So on Sunday, he pitched a nine inning victory for the great Camden team in Fairview, New Jersey. On Monday, Labor Day, he travelled with the Camden club to Orange, New Jersey, where he set the great Paterson Silk Stockings on their ears for another nine innings. *These were his 64th and 65th wins of the season!*

By 4 o'clock on Tuesday morning, old Rube was out on his milk route, doing his duty to keep the customers happy after the long weekend. He would take on the Cardinals after a full day's work.

That night, the atmosphere in the neighborhood was electric. For those lucky enough to get inside, the highlight of the night came shortly after Pepper Martin, The Wild Hoss of the Osage, touched the Milkman for a single. All Philadelphians knew that the Rube had a smooth move to first base. He and Holstein baited Martin a little by giving him an extra step. Then, death arrived for the Pepper when Rube rifled the ball to Holstein, who in deer-like fashion ran down the runner as he headed for the keystone sack.

There wasn't much more excitement in the game. Rube registered victory number 66 by shutting out the Cardinals on four hits, as the two future Hall of Famers, Medwick and Bottomley, were hitless.

After the game, some people made the excuse that the major leaguers were not accustomed to portable lights. This was true. But Rube, after two big weekend wins and a long day of work, had easily beaten baseball's reigning World Champions. No excuses can lessen the magnitude of such an achievement. Rube had risen to the heights. The King of the Sandlots, he remains to this day one of Philadelphia's greatest legends.

Cardinals

		R	H	O	A	E	
Flowers	ss	0	1	1	2	0	
Medwick	cf	0	0	0	0	0	
Reese	2b	0	0	2	1	0	
Bottomley	1b	0	0	4	1	0	
Martin	3b	0	2	0	0	0	
Collins	rf	0	1	2	0	0	
Puccinelli	lf	0	0	2	0	1	
Wilson	c	0	0	5	0	0	
Stout	p	0	0	0	1	0	
Mancuso	c	0	0	7	0	0	
Blades	rf	0	0	1	0	0	
Johnson	p	0	0	0	0	0	
Wares	ph	0	0	0	0	0	
Totals		**0**	**4**	**24**	**5**	**1**	

Legion

		R	H	O	A	E	
Eberts	3b	0	0	1	0	0	
Spalding	rf	0	0	1	0	0	
Muffler	2b	0	2	1	2	1	
Sothern	cf	0	0	1	0	0	
Roetz	ss	2	3	3	1	0	
Lohr	lf	0	2	1	0	0	
Holstein	1b	1	2	12	0	0	
Sharkey	c	0	0	7	0	0	
Chambers	p	0	0	0	7	0	
Totals		**3**	**9**	**27**	**10**	**1**	

St. Louis   000 000 000 - 0 4 1
Legion   010 200 00x - 3 9 1

Les Tietje

Steve Smart

Some things never change. Something really special, like getting a chance to play baseball in the major leagues, has always been a great dream of men. No matter if your name was McGraw or Manush.

That's the way it is today, and that's the way it was in 1933 when Les Tietje (Tee-Gee) got his chance to pitch for the Chicago White Sox.

By the time his career ended in the majors, Les had been dealt to the Browns of St. Louis. Along the way there were great times and the other kind. I had a lot of questions about those times when I visited Les and his wife Bonnie in their beautiful farm home near Rochester, Minnesota. The Tietjes have been retired there for twenty years. Les and Bonnie sat on their couch recollecting stories about life in the big leagues.

Like most of the communities around north Iowa and southern Minnesota, we had our local baseball team in Sumner, Iowa, which I played on. It wasn't organized or anything, you know, but we played weekends against one another for bragging rights. The bigger cities had organized teams and they'd play exhibition games against our local teams for extra money. I guess somebody must have thought I had a pretty good arm, because other towns would ask me to pitch some of their Sunday games against those traveling teams.

It was 1931, our Sumner team made a trip to Waterloo to play an exhibition game against the Class A White Sox farm team, the White Hawks. I pitched nine innings and we beat them 3–2. Well, we get home, and three days

Steve Smart works in the Neuroradiology Department at the Mayo Clinic.

later they call and want me to come down to Waterloo and sign a contract. They offered me $150 a month. Now, I was making more in Sumner—fifty bucks a week, working and playing ball. But this was Organized Baseball. I pitched the rest of 1931 and part of '32 with Waterloo, going 9–11. Part way through '32, they sent me to Dallas in the tough Texas League. Some good players came out of that league. Johnny Whitehead and Zeke Bonura were a couple of my teammates at Dallas. I'll tell you, Zeke was a character. His dad would send him a big check to cover his expenses so he could put his money in the bank. His old man was a banana peddler in New Orleans. He had a fleet of banana boats between New Orleans and South America. He was a millionaire. I made $350 a month with Dallas and went 14–3 the rest of '32 and all of 1933. September of '33, the White Sox called Joe Chamberlain, an infielder, and me up to Chicago.

Imagine, a kid sitting on a major league bench with Jimmy Dykes and Al Simmons and all those other stars you'd heard about, well I'll tell you, it was exciting. We were going to play a doubleheader against the Yankees at Comiskey when our manager, Lew Fonseca, came up and told me I was going to pitch the second game. Red Ruffing was pitching for the Yankees that game, and well, I was very fortunate to get a few runs early and we beat them 4–3 on three hits. A week later the team traveled east to Philadelphia and Mr. Fonseca gave me another start, this time against the A's. Wouldn't you know it, I threw a 5–0 shutout on a two-hitter. In that game by the way, I got my only hit of the season—a double with the bases loaded to knock in three runs.

I'll tell you something funny. When word got back to Sumner that I was going to pitch against the New York

Yankees, everyone tuned in the Des Moines radio station that was broadcasting the game to hear Ronald Reagan do the play-by-play. My folks said he never did pronounce my name right, but of course he was getting it over the ticker tape.

I got invited to the 1934 spring training camp in Pasadena with the White Sox where I was reunited with another Dallas teammate, Whitlow Wyatt. He was a fastball pitcher—really fast. He was used as a relief pitcher with the White Sox, but later became famous, of course, as a starter with the Brooklyn Dodgers. He had a real rubber arm then. He could go three, four days in a row throwing nothing but fastballs, and I don't think the speed varied one or two miles per hour from the first day to the last.

Bonnie and I had gotten married in '34 and we made arrangements, once we knew we had made the team, with Whitlow and his wife Edna along with the Applings, Luke and Faye, to rent in an apartment complex on the South Side near the ballpark to save some money and for convenience.

I guess my closest friend on that team was Luke Appling. What a wonderful man. I don't think today's shortstops could carry Luke's glove. The closest I've seen is Greg Gagne with the Twins. But oh, could Luke hit—.312, .308 every year. We really had fun with Luke.

I remember a gorgeous brand new Buick that Luke got in 1934. Dual horns on the fenders, chrome all over. It

was as big as a hearse. We went to this night club just south of Chicago. A real tough place. We didn't know if it was vandals or hoods or what, but while we were in the place they stripped it down, took the tires, took the horns, just destroyed it. Oh, he was mad!

He liked his horses. Whenever we had a rain-out, right to the race track we'd go. We never bet too much, but there was this one guy—Joe Heving, a pitcher. I never saw anybody bet all the time like that, every day, every day. If he couldn't get to the track, there was a bookie shop right next to the hotel where he could go over and bet. The only one I ever saw that could outdo Joe was Hornsby. The day he got released from St. Louis, he won 37,000 bucks at the track. He wouldn't bet a two dollar bet, it was always $100, $100, $100 across the board. Four or five horses.

Part way through the '34 season, the brass fired Lew Fonseca and made Jimmy Dykes player–manager. Dykes had come over to the Sox from the A's with Al Simmons and George Earnshaw. He was a smart baseball man. A Connie Mack boy, I'll tell you. Probably the smartest guy on the team though, as far as the pitchers were concerned, was Herold 'Muddy' Ruel. He was one of the great catchers. He caught Walter Johnson in his prime. For us, he'd catch maybe two games a week, then come down to the bullpen and set with us young pitchers and teach us to be pitchers and not just throwers. We'd

Les Tietje

NBL

watch the other pitchers during the game and he'd explain why you would do something in this situation and then do another thing now. He'd say, 'Now's a good time to change-up, pull the string on your fastball, you've got him guessing. Watch their feet and you got 'em.'

My best pitch was the change-up. I had good luck against the big hitters—Ruth, Foxx and them. That's how I got those guys out. You could feel the wind when they took those big swings. Chicago had an outstanding rotation of starters in those years: Ted Lyons, George Earnshaw, Milt Gaston and 'Sad' Sam Jones. The thing I remember about Sam Jones was that he never threw over to first base. He'd just step off the mound and look 'em back. He had a real quick move to home. Never lifted his front foot up.

I was a spot starter with the White Sox but even with their great staff, I figured time was on my side. I was wrong. After spending spring training with the White Sox in 1936, I was traded to the St. Louis Browns. It was a hot, humid place to play ball, the last place I wanted to be traded. It was September '36 they had to send me home. I had gone from 185 to 135 pounds. That was the year it was so hot in St. Louis, people were dropping like flies. You'd open the paper and another twenty or thirty people had died.

I had been bothered by arthritis on and off but in 1936, because of the heat and humidity I think, it really got worse. During the All-Star break that year, I came home to Iowa where Bonnie's father and I did some fence work in a river. Standing in cold water all day. By the time I took the train back to St. Louis, well, I had gotten so bad they had to help me off the train to get to the hotel. It started in my knees and hips, then went to my shoulders, elbows and wrists. They couldn't find any reason or cure for it. They prescribed a regimen of vitamins and cod liver oil, but I never completely got over the stiffness.

Some days were better than others pitching for the Browns, but I certainly made a lot of friends in St. Louis. But I'll tell you one guy nobody liked and that was our manager, Rogers Hornsby. Now there was a real p-r-i-c-k. We had a catcher, Rollie Hemsley, he liked to drink. I'm surprised Rollie didn't kill Hornsby. Hornsby fined him every damn trip we'd go on—1,500 bucks in 1936 alone, and that was a lot of money in those days. With Hornsby, except for his *Racing Form*s, there were no newspapers, no movies, no beer, nothing. Women and horses, that was his downfall.

Jim Bottomley took over for Hornsby, then Gabby Street took over from Sunny Jim. We had fun in St. Louis. They had a pretty fair pitching staff too. Oral Hildebrand, he was a tough one. He'd just as soon hit you between the eyes than look at you. There was a kid, Jim Walkup, gosh we had some fun with him. Hornsby had a rule, if you got two strikes on a guy, you'd waste a pitch. He'd fine you twenty-five bucks if you didn't. Jim had two strikes on Gehrig and he threw one right down the middle. Gehrig

hit the ball to center for an out, but I can still hear Jim out there shouting, 'Don't hit it. Don't swing.' Hornsby fined him twenty-five bucks.

I'll tell you another character we had, Bobo Newsom. He was really something. He talked a lot, but he could back it up, too. He had been around a while by the time he got back to the Browns in '38. He was another one of those rubber arms. He could pitch two games in one day. If he didn't win the first game of a doubleheader, he'd ask to pitch the second.

Travel was bad. We would leave Boston at five o'clock in the afternoon. Ride all night long, all the next day, until eleven o'clock at night to get to St. Louis. Then play a game the next day. No air-conditioning. Windows wide open. Coal dust flying in your face. I'd like to see these guys today, with their salaries, try to play ball with all that.

My arm never did come back to form. It would show promise in the spring but the arthritis would flare up in the summer, making my pitches ineffective.

In 1939, Mike Kelley of the Minneapolis Millers bought my contract. I went to spring training with them but requested a trade to San Antonio, hoping the dry heat would help the arm. It did some, too. I went 17–10 with San Antonio, but that summer, Bonnie and I became parents for the first time. We decided that after the season, it would be a good time for me to retire and move back to Iowa.

Joe L. Brown, son of comedian Joe E. Brown, was general manager of the Waterloo team in 1940. He asked me to do some coaching and throwing on the side. I really enjoyed working with the young talent and staying involved in organized ball. By 1942, Joe L. was the GM of the Pittsburgh Pirates, and wanted me to be a Midwest scout. But by then, I had signed a contract with the U.S. Government to deliver 1,200 cases of eggs a week to the armed forces, so I had to tell him I was through with baseball.

We had a fleet of trucks we'd send out to the chicken farmers we had signed up to produce eggs for us. We had thirty-two farmers we collected from. The trucks then would take the eggs to the train depot to be packaged and sent overseas. The farmers used to give us their gas ration cards to run trucks for pick-up. Actually, we stayed in the egg business until 1962 when I got a job in Rochester at Crenlo Manufacturing Co. where I eventually retired as a supervisor.

It's lovely out here in the country and we're lucky to have two of our children living on either side of us. Bonnie and I leave Minnesota every fall, though, to drive to our winter home in Texas. We both love to golf and we live right next to a course. On our way back north in the spring, we would always swing through spring training and visit the Applings on our way back.

I guess I've been a lucky man. Had a really special life. My wife, my family, and a chance to play major league baseball.

The Chicago School of Baseball Writing

Tom Nawrocki

In his time, Henry Chadwick was known as the Father of Baseball, and the title fits him as well as anyone. Originator of the box score and block-style standings, codifier of rules and statistics, grand proselytizer for the nascent sport, Chadwick was indispensable to the early growth of the game. He could also be rightfully considered the father of American baseball journalism, having written a published report of a baseball game as early as 1858. Chadwick not only filed daily game stories but edited annual guides and wrote extensively on baseball's history, strategies, techniques and ethics.

Any treatise on baseball in the 19th century will rely heavily on Chadwick. Harold Seymour's *Baseball: The Early Years* cites him eighteen separate times. Chadwick saw his first game at the hallowed Elysian Fields in Hoboken, New Jersey, in 1848, accompanied the Washington Nationals on their legendary 1867 tour of the Midwest, and covered the Brooklyn Superbas on Opening Day, 1908. His influence cannot be overstated, yet his legacy has become somehow understated. Although he churned out an amazing quantity of text, Chadwick's works are rarely anthologized; indeed, he is seldom quoted at length. For while Henry Chadwick was peerless in his knowledge of the game, his writing can be charitably described as colorless. Historian David Voigt has written of Chadwick's "stilted style [filled with] repetitive verbosities." His game stories tended to begin with a description of the teams' standing and an estimate of attendance. Here is the lead for an 1877 game report under

the headline "An Exciting Baseball Contest": "The seventh game of the series between the Boston and Brooklyn nines took place yesterday on the Union Grounds in the presence of a large crowd of spectators, considerable interest being taken in the match, owing to the position occupied by the Boston nine in the pennant race." Chadwick then continued into his recap of the game, inning by painstaking inning. The score can be determined by peeking ahead to the box score below the story or by toting up the runs as they occur in the game summary; Chadwick clearly expects his readers to pay attention.

And if they pay attention, those fans will be rewarded with a wealth of insight. From 1884: "The play of the Brooklyns in these games has shown pretty conclusively that it is not from lack of good material that they have not succeeded. The players are there, but not the team work to make their play effective." He sees everything with a careful, knowledgeable eye but conveys little of the excitement or fun inherent in the game he devoted his life to.

Chadwick championed baseball purity, if not minimalism; he once called a fifteen-inning scoreless tie between Syracuse and St. Louis "the finest game of ball ever played." In 1886 he reported, "In the National League the Providence club was twice shut out without a base hit, once by Ferguson of the Philadelphia club and once by Clarkson of the Chicago club. . . . These are the most remarkable pitching feats of the season." No-hitters had not yet acquired the drama and notoriety with which they are associated today. Chadwick appreciated the spare, unspectacular beauty of these games, and this esthetic carried over into his daily reporting.

Tom Nawrocki is an editor at Rolling Stone *magazine. He lives in Hoboken, NJ.*

In a sense, Chadwick was just following the fashion of his day, but he was also setting that fashion as the leading scribe of the times. Other papers imitated Chadwick's dry, information-filled style, as this 1886 example from the *Chicago Inter Ocean* demonstrates: "The team presented by Captain Anson had particular reference to the effectiveness of Baldwin, Detroit's left-handed pitcher, and Dalrymple and Gore, both left-hand batters, were accordingly laid off, Flynn and Ryan taking care of left and center fields." The attorney-like prose somewhat disguises the fact that the writer is describing a very early instance of platooning. The level of information provided is surprisingly sophisticated, yet the approach is unlikely to appeal to anyone but a serious fan.

By the mid-1880s, a Chicago newspaper editor named Butch White decided that baseball could be made attractive to a wider audience. He was buoyed in this decision by the sterling success of the Chicago White Stockings, who in 1886 took their fifth pennant in seven years. White's *Daily News* had merely printed box scores up to this point, so he did not have a seasoned reporter to send to the games. He chose a nineteen-year-old writer named Finley Peter Dunne to cover Cap Anson and the White Stockings for the *Daily News* during the summer of 1887. Around the same time, the *Chicago Herald* assigned Charlie Seymour to cover baseball, and the *Inter Ocean* sent Len Washburn; each was, like Dunne, a relative baseball novice but a hungry young reporter able to make something special out of rote game coverage. "None of them knew much about technical baseball; nor was an intimate knowledge of the sport considered necessary," wrote the Chicago sportswriting legend Hugh Fullerton in a 1928 *Saturday Evening Post* piece, "The Fellows Who Made the Game." "The idea was to write interesting stories about the games and the players."

The change was immediately noticeable. Dunne's lead from July 1, 1887, contrasts stunningly with Chadwick:

> The Chicagos lost a game yesterday by the thickness of a coat of paint. They had the game comfortably won with tallies to spare when Schock of the Washingtons went to bat in the ninth inning. He scraped a fly off the Congress street wall with a fly from his bat and won the game. The ball alighted on the top of the wall and for a short time seemed undecided whether to roll inside and let Sullivan fall over it or drop on the outside. The absence of a coat of paint, for which President Spalding is responsible, rolled it into the street.

Washburn, a general-assignment reporter who had previously covered horse racing and prizefights, became known for his light style and masterful imagery: Harry Staley's pitches "wandered down toward the plate like a boy on his way to school;" Ned Williamson's hot smash ripped through a poorly mowed infield "sounding like the

hired man eating celery." Seymour became known for his storytelling; he was perhaps the first reporter to incorporate the players' opinions into his spot reporting. Seymour and Washburn between them set about inventing a new vocabulary for the game, coining (or at least popularizing) terms like shutout, initial sack and circus catch. (However, one term that Seymour or Dunne is often credited with inventing, southpaw, has been traced by Paul Dickson to *The Sporting Life* magazine in 1885, before either of the two had ever covered a baseball game.)

Among baseball people the credit for developing the new relaxed, humorous style often goes to Washburn, who lasted longest as a baseball writer and who was ultimately the most influential. Fullerton insisted in 1928 that Washburn was the one who initiated the change. (Complicating matters is the fact that none of the stories of the time were bylined.) While Dunne's 1887 pieces are recognizably his own, because the *Inter Ocean*'s style developed more slowly, we have no way of knowing exactly when Washburn came aboard. The *Inter Ocean*'s 1886 stories (as cited above) are certainly not Washburn's, which would date his emergence at the beginning of the 1887 season, with Seymour and Dunne following shortly thereafter.

If the chronology is correct, then Washburn's initial efforts toward a comic voice were tentative. The *Inter Ocean*'s baseball reporting throughout 1887 hews fairly closely to tradition, with an occasional punchy line or attempt at lightheartedness thrown in. From August 2: "Williamson caught Daily's popped-up fly with his eyes closed, it was so easy." Although that is hardly a sentence that Henry Chadwick would have written, it pales next to this from Pete Dunne, an off-day report (July 29) on heartthrob Mike "King" Kelly, who had been sold from Chicago to Boston for the '87 season, and his bunion problems: "Mr. Kelly's bunion was minced by a prominent jeweler, who paid $125 for it and sold the pieces at 50 cents apiece to sentimental young Boston women to wear on their bangles. Mr. Harris assures us that no Boston girl is considered au fait unless she flaunts a sample of Mr. Kelly's bunion on her bracelet."

Dunne lasted but a year on the baseball beat, so his influence on sportswriting in general was minimal. But his influence on Len Washburn, who went on to cast a great shadow in the field, was profound. By 1891, Washburn was spinning comic masterpieces on the sports pages, packed with more baseball detail than Dunne's work ever was. (Pittsburgh shortstop Doggie Miller, more regularly a catcher, "covered about as much ground as a woodshed, and threw to first like a drunkard with a cork leg.") For that he deserves credit for helping to revolutionize the sports page. But Finley Peter Dunne fired the opening shot.

The Chicago school was quick to catch on around the country, although the eastern cities in the league were slower to adapt to the new style, New York then as now being the media capital of the nation and suspicious of trends that develop outside its borders. But Cincinnati became the second city for innovative reporting; among the local papers' alums were the legendary editor Harry Weldon and the future American League president Ban Johnson. "Until after the Chicago trio of geniuses made baseball interesting to readers," wrote Fullerton in 1928, "the accounts of Cincinnati games were as drab as cricket reporting. Afterward all the Redland scribes, consciously or unconsciously, followed the new system." In 1887 the *Boston Globe* hired former NL first baseman Tim Murnane as a baseball reporter. He proceeded to file stories consisting almost entirely of slang while also making use of the deep technical knowledge enjoyed by Chadwick. The *Washington Evening Star* didn't carry any baseball news at all in 1886; by 1892 it was running such notes as "Uncle Can't-See-for-the-Life-of-Me-How-We-Get-Beat Anson is the latest appellation by which Chicago's venerable first baseman is known."

The *Philadelphia Inquirer* provides a good before-and-after picture. Here is an entire game report from July 1, 1886:

> The Pittsburgs [the Steel City didn't reliably take its final "h" for a few years yet] won another easy game from the Athletics this afternoon, making the third successive defeat for the latter club by the home nine. Atkisson [Al Atkinson] went in to pitch for the visitors, but had one of his fingers hurt by the first hit, and Kennedy was substituted. The Pittsburgs immediately jumped on to his delivery and batted him for 16 [hits], with a total of 22 bases. Galvin was also batted hard, but the hits were scattered. Larkin's batting was the feature of the game, which was too much one-sided to be interesting to the three thousand spectators.

Compare that with the first paragraph of a story from the same paper on August 11, 1892:

> The Phillies added another victory to their list yesterday, and this time the champions of the first division were the victims. The Bostonians evidently expected to strike a snap, but they were badly fooled. Before the game Manager Selee was heard to remark: "We ought to win this game dead easy. Clements is laid up with a bad arm and the Phillies are also without the services of a third baseman, as Reilly had his head caved in by a pitched ball on Monday," but when the Phillies came on the field there was a man behind the bat that knew a thing or two about catching, and skipping around the third bag was someone who looked very much like Charley

Reilly. When the cranks on the bleachers noticed Charley they set up a howl of delight, but later in the game, when he began to cut off base hits and make lightning throws to first, the applause was deafening.

Charles Dryden, at one time commonly called the Mark Twain of Baseball, was one of the Chicago school's prime acolytes, hired by Finley Peter Dunne after Dunne moved out of the press box. Dryden spun his baseball stories for at least ten different papers from New York to San Francisco, and his itinerancy is probably all that keeps him from being more recognized today. William Phelon, a second-generation Chicago reporter who joined the *Chicago Morning News* in 1899, was still at that late date feeling the effects of the class of '87. In 1908, he told *Baseball Magazine*, "Washburn brought the comedy portion of baseball writing to its pinnacles, and today, every press-stand is full of keen-witted, clever boys, who make their stuff entertaining and interesting, but the grade of their copy has not advanced since 1892, while it is ten times better than the dull descriptions that were published in 1895."

The triumvirate that laid down the benchmark for contemporary sports reporting was destined not to be long for the field. In January of 1888, Dunne was hired away by the *Chicago Times* as a political reporter. He would go on to literary fame as the creator of the archetypal Irish Chicagoan, barstool philosopher Mr. Dooley. Charlie Seymour was deemed too important to cover only baseball, and before long was reporting on sports on only the most momentous occasions.

Washburn, the one who really developed a new level of baseball reporting, was the most tragic story. In 1891, returning to Chicago from Wisconsin after covering a prize fight, he was killed when his train jumped the tracks and plowed into a signal tower. He had spent just five years covering the sport, but in those five years he became, as anthologist Charles Einstein later wrote, "one of the funniest baseball writers of all."

Henry Chadwick continued his work, oblivious of the new style, until his death in 1908. As Fullerton said: "He never quite adapted himself to the lighter strain and continued to write rather painful, if accurate, accounts of games almost to the end." And though the influence of the Chicago school permeated the hyperactive slang of the 1920s—developing into the statelier Grantland Rice style ("Outlined against a blue-gray October sky, the Four Horsemen rode again")—there were rumbles even in Chadwick's time that the fun was already seeping out. In the year of Chadwick's death, Peter Vroom wrote: "Many complain that baseball writers take things too seriously, that the old school of Len Washburn and others made things more entertaining and breezy."

Billy Goodman

Jim Sumner

Every successful baseball team needs a good utilityman or two, someone who can fill in at any one of several positions when a regular gets hurt or needs some rest. A valuable man to have around, but by definition not a star. Once in a while, a utilityman may set a higher standard. But none has approached the marks set in 1950 by Billy Goodman, a man his manager Steve O'Neill called "a one-man bench."

Billy Goodman had some definite shortcomings as a professional baseball player. He had average speed and a mediocre throwing arm. A slimly built player—sportswriter Al Hirshberg once wrote that he was "built like an undernourished ribbon clerk"—Goodman had little home run punch. He hit only 19 home runs in a 16-year big league career. Yet the left-handed hitter could spray line drives to any corner of the field. Pitcher Tex Hughson claimed that Goodman had a "seeing-eye bat." He could hit lefties or righties, power pitchers or finesse pitchers and he was a sure-handed fielder, albeit one with limited range. He also had the perfect temperament for a utilityman. Self-effacing and modest, Goodman was a consummate team player—a breed in short supply in the fractious world of the 1950s Red Sox.

Goodman was born in Cabarrus County, North Carolina on March 22, 1926. Like so many southern players of that time he grew up on a farm. His father had played in semipro leagues in the area and he encouraged his sons to play baseball—after the completion of their chores, of course. Although Goodman starred at Winecoff High

Jim Sumner is historian/curator with the North Carolina Museum of History. He is the author of numerous books and articles on North Carolina sports history.

School, he learned additional lessons in the semipro textile leagues of the area. The best of these leagues were fiercely competitive, dominated by strong men who cherished their relatively privileged positions in a depression economy. Yet the teenage Goodman excelled among these tough customers. When he signed with the Atlanta Crackers of the Southern Association before the 1944 season, he was already a skilled hitter. He batted .336 in his rookie campaign, then spent 1945 in the navy, where he contracted a strange jungle fungus that bothered him off and on for the next several years. He returned to the Crackers in the middle of the 1946 season and batted a sterling .389. The Red Sox purchased his contract for a reported $75,000 and sent him to Louisville, where he played outfield and shortstop in 1947, batting .340.

Goodman made the Red Sox for good in the spring of 1948. He started at first base in 1948 and 1949 and batted in the .300 range both seasons. However, by the end of the 1949 season Goodman had hit only a single home run in almost 1,000 at bats; he obviously was not the power hitter Boston would have liked at first. Making Goodman's tenure even more tenuous at the beginning of 1950 was the shadow of huge, young Walt Dropo, who was tearing up the minors.

Goodman and Dropo were competing for playing time at first base on a team that boasted considerable offensive ability. Boston's undisputed batting leader was left fielder Ted Williams, the best hitter in the game. Joining Williams were such threats as Vern Stephens, Bobby Doerr, Dom DiMaggio, and Al Zarilla. Boston would finish the 1950 season with a .302 team batting average and would score more than 1,000 runs. The slugging Red Sox had won the American League pennant in 1946 and had just

Billy Goodman

when Ted Williams fractured his left elbow making a leaping catch against the wall to retire Ralph Kiner in the All-Star game. The injury was believed not to be serious at the time. Indeed Williams received a quick arm massage and continued to play. After the game it was announced that Williams had "jammed his left elbow" and would be able to resume play after the break. Williams knew better, however. When the pain got worse, he went in for X-rays, which revealed a badly shattered elbow. Surgery was performed immediately, but there was no guarantee Williams would be able to return before 1951. At the time of his injury the Red Sox were in fourth place at 42–35. They trailed the league-leading Tigers by eight games, the Yankees by five, and the Indians by 3-1/2. Without their superstar, it seemed there was little realistic chance the Red Sox could contend for the pennant.

This would be Goodman's biggest challenge. Filling the shoes of the Splendid Splinter was an order of magnitude more difficult than filling in for a Stephens or a Doerr, as talented as those players were. This substitution would be for months, not weeks or days. In addition, Goodman faced the difficulties of playing Fenway's notorious left field wall on a regular basis. Manager O'Neill (who had replaced Joe McCarthy early in the season) evidently had his doubts, because he gave the job to Clyde Vollmer for a few short days. Vollmer proved unequal to the task and Goodman was asked to take over in left field.

Although he clearly lacked Williams' prodigious home run power, Goodman did a spectacular job. In one memorable game, on August 28, his three-run double capped a 14–13 Boston victory over the pitching-rich Cleveland Indians, who blew a 12–1 lead. Goodman finished August batting a league-leading .370. He also played The Wall competently. Most important, the Red Sox were winning. At the end of August they were only 2-1/2 games behind the first place Yankees. Their record at that time was 78–49, 36–14 since Williams' injury.

The race would get even tighter. On September 6, an overflow crowd of 34,995 jammed Fenway Park to see Goodman go 2-for-4 and score three times as Boston thrashed the hated Yankees 11–2. The loss pulled Boston within 2-1/2 games of New York, two behind the Tigers. The next day Dropo homered twice to lead Boston to a 10–8 victory over New York. On the 9th Boston took a pair from the Philadelphia Athletics 6–3 and 11–3 to pull within 1-1/2 of Detroit, only 1/2 behind New York. When Tom Wright's three-run double in the eighth inning propelled Boston to a 6–2 victory over Philadelphia on September 10, the Red Sox had closed to within a single game of the league-leading Tigers.

Goodman had become the toast of the baseball world. He was featured not only in such obvious publications as *The Sporting News*, but also more mainstream publications, such as *Time* magazine. He reacted with characteristic modesty, telling one North Carolina re-

missed in 1948 and 1949. The Sox had every expectation of competing for the 1950 title.

Boston demonstrated this fearsome batting prowess in early June, when they scored forty-nine runs in consecutive starts against the lowly St. Louis Browns. They did this without Goodman, who was on the bench after starting the season at first base. He had chipped an ankle sliding into first base beating out a bunt on April 30 and had missed three weeks. By the time he got back Dropo had been promoted from the minors and had taken over the first base position. Dropo would go on to drive in a league high 144 runs. It was obvious that if Goodman was going to play, it would not be at first base. Yet opportunities kept presenting themselves. He replaced Vern Stephens at shortstop for one game when Stephens was ill, then moved to third base for two weeks when Johnny Pesky got hurt. He batted .455 filling in for Pesky. Doerr got hurt in June and Goodman filled in at second for five games, hitting safely in all five. Goodman showed a remarkable ability to maintain his hitting stroke despite the roller-coaster ride in the field. However, Boston's habitually mediocre pitching staff kept them behind the league-leading Tigers and Yankees.

On July 11 Boston's season took a dramatic detour

porter that "it's great, but you have to be lucky. If you don't get the luck you can't do it." When Williams began working out for a September return, oddsmakers made Boston the favorite for the pennant and Red Sox fans cleared their calendars for the World Series.

Williams made his first trip back, pinch-hitting, on the 7th. He returned to the starting line-up on September 15 with a vengeance. He went 4-for-6, with a home run and three runs batted in, to lead Boston to a 12–9 win over the Browns. Goodman went 2-for-5 at third base. At this point the Red Sox were a game behind the Yanks, 1-½ behind the Tigers. During Williams' absence from the starting line-up, Boston had gone 44–17. Surely with him back they would pull away from the rest of the league.

Of course, Red Sox fans know better. Just as Boston confounded the experts by gaining ground without Williams, they confounded them the last three weeks of the season by falling off the pace with him. Two losses in mid-September to the usually inept St. Louis Browns didn't help matters. Perhaps more important in the long run was a late surge by the Yankees, whose already strong pitching staff was bolstered by the late season acquisition of young lefthanded Eddie Ford, not yet widely known by his distinctive nickname, "Whitey." Ford's 9–1 record enabled the Yankees to pull away not only from Boston but also from Detroit. The Red Sox hung tough but lost some crucial games. A late-season twin-bill loss to Cleveland's great righthanders Bob Lemon and Early Wynn by scores of 6–3 and 7–1 was critical. On September 23 and 24, New York took games from Boston by scores of 8–0 and 9–5 to drop the Sox four games back and effectively put them out of the race. Goodman did not play in the first contest and went 1-for-5 in the second.

In fact, Goodman's playing status had become something of a controversy. While the three contenders were fighting it out for first place, Goodman had opened a substantial lead in the batting race over runner-up George Kell, Detroit's standout third baseman and the 1949 batting titleist. Sportswriters across the country, especially in Boston, began to refer to what became known as "O'Neill's dilemma." The United Press compared this dilemma to be "sort of like having to decide between double-thick sirloin steak or filet mignon." How do you bench a .370 hitter, they asked? Johnny Pesky solved the problem by offering to sit down to let Goodman play at third. Flabbergasted sportswriters, accustomed to a more me-first attitude on the part of the Red Sox, hopefully— and as it turned out erroneously—declared this unselfish act the beginning of a new age of Red Sox harmony.

Goodman played through a bad head cold in the middle of August, and saw his weight drop from 160 pounds at the start of the season to 145 pounds by September. By September 16, though, he had the at bats he

needed for the batting title. With the title locked up, he sat out the final week, only pinch-hitting twice in the last eight games.

The Red Sox concluded the campaign in third place, four games behind the pennant winning Yankees. Goodman slumped slightly in the last weeks but still finished with a .354 average, 14 points ahead of Kell. He scored 91 runs and drove in 68. The "one man bench" played 45 games in the outfield (the most he would ever play there), 27 at third base, 21 at first base, five at second base, and only one at shortstop. His contribution to Boston's run at the title was recognized when sportswriters voted him second to New York's Phil Rizzuto (another scrawny guy with no power) in the American League Most Valuable Player Award voting.

Goodman never duplicated his marvelous 1950 season. However, he played well enough through the 1950s to demonstrate conclusively that it was no fluke. He even found a regular spot of sorts. Doerr retired after the 1951 season and Goodman became the more-or-less regular second baseman, although Boston managers continued to experiment with other second basemen and continued to play Goodman at other positions. Wherever he played, Goodman always managed to hit around .300.

Boston traded Goodman to the Baltimore Orioles early in the 1957 season. The next year he was traded to the Chicago White Sox. In 1959, at the age of 33, Goodman platooned at third base for the White Sox and batted .250. More important, he was able to fulfill his last baseball ambition, playing in a World Series. He batted .231 as the White Sox fell to the Los Angeles Dodgers in six games.

Goodman finished his big league career in 1962 with the expansion Houston Colt .45s, later Astros. He stayed in the organization as a manager and coach for several years. In 1963, he returned to his native state and managed the Durham Bulls in the Carolina League. Among his Bulls that year was a 19-year-old rookie named Joe Morgan, who presumably learned something about playing second base from his manager. Even as he was approaching the age of 40, Goodman proved he could still hit. As a player-manager for the Bulls, he hit .354 in 1963 and .325 in 1964. Not surprisingly, he filled in wherever his manager needed him. Goodman completed his managerial career in 1965 in the Florida State League. He died in Florida on October 1, 1984.

Billy Goodman played at least 100 major league games at four different positions. He finished his big league career with a batting average of exactly .300, a mark every major leaguer shoots at but few reach. Taken in its entirety, it was a fine career, but his 1950 season, when he filled in for Ted Williams, Johnny Pesky, Bobby Doerr, and Vern Stephens; won the batting title, and finished second in the MVP voting, set a standard for all utilitymen to shoot for.

"XX" and Hoosier Chuck

Steve Krevisky

In 1933, Philadelphia had not only one Triple Crown winner, but two. Jimmie Foxx of the Philadelphia Athletics and Chuck Klein of the crosstown Phillies both led their leagues in home runs, runs batted in, and batting average—the only time in major league history that one town could lay claim to two Crowns.

Coming into the 1933 season, the A's had completed a five-year run during which they sandwiched two second-place finishes around three straight pennants. By today's rules, Foxx would have won the Triple Crown in 1932, because Dale Alexander, who won the batting title with .367 in a season split between Detroit and Boston, wouldn't have had enough at-bats. Foxx had had a tremendous year, blasting 58 homers, with 169 RBIs, a .364 batting average, 151 runs scored, a .469 on-base average and a .749 slugging average.

While the Phillies didn't enjoy the A's success, Klein was coming off four consecutive years of 200-plus hits, two straight years of leading the league in home runs, and three consecutive years of leading in runs scored. While he was undoubtedly helped by the small confines of Baker Bowl, whereas Foxx played in the much bigger Shibe Park, Klein was at the height of his considerable powers as a run producer.

As the 1933 season began, both Foxx and the Athletics got off to slow starts. Their April 20 home opener, however, was a resounding success. Foxx received a local MVP trophy before the game, and the mayor threw out the first ball. Then the A's got down to work. Lefty Grove

Steve Krevisky is a math professor at Middlesex Community Technical College in Middletown, CT. He is also the editor of The Left Field Baseball Book. *His article, "Unusual Extra Base Hits," appeared in the 1989* Baseball Research Journal. *He is a Yankee fan in spite of George.*

pitched the A's to an 8–1 triumph, and XX belted his first two homers of the season. He went 3-for-3, scored three times and drove in five runs. Both of his circuit clouts cleared the leftfield pavilion. All of this action in a game that lasted just an hour and 45 minutes!

Klein drilled his first home run of the season on April 24 against the Braves. He got three hits in a game that the Phils won, 6-5 in 12 innings. On this same day, Jimmie blasted his third home run of the year, tying him with the Yankees' Lou Gehrig for the league lead. (Sunny Jim Bottomley of the Reds paced the NL with two). This round tripper, drilled into Fenway's right-center field bleachers, accounted for one of his five hits for the day and gave him seven RBIs in a 16–10 victory over the Red Sox.

Klein had a tremendous day on May 10, popping three home runs in a doubleheader against the Reds. This gave him six for the season, giving him the NL lead over Wally Berger and Gabby Hartnett, who each had five.

On May 20, Foxx broke loose from what had become an early-season slump, and ripped his fifth and sixth home runs, both to right field. He picked up four RBIs in the process. He followed with his seventh four-bagger three days later. The A's, barely above .500, were still only 3-1/2 games behind the first-place Yankees. The Phils were already in the cellar, 9-1/2 behind the front-running Pirates.

Hoosier Chuck hit for the cycle on May 26 against the Cards. After the game, he was a home run behind Berger, who had 10. His .338 was fifth, behind Pepper Martin's .369. Klein led the league with 38 RBIs and 13 doubles.

The Maryland Broadback really rolled on June 8, powering three home runs in one game against the Bronx Bombers, all against Lefty Gomez (my father's childhood hero). Foxx scored four runs, drove in five, and enjoyed the A's first win against the Yankees in their ninth try this year. XX now had 11 four-baggers on the season. Ruth and Gehrig also homered in this game. The Depression-battered fans in the Stadium really got their precious money's worth this day!

Since Jimmie had homered in his last at-bat on June 7, before touching up Gomez in his first three at bats here, he had homered in four consecutive plate appearances. He'd totaled 10 RBIs with this barrage. In the home-run derby, Ruth led with 12, with Gehrig and Foxx right behind with 11. In the NL, Klein and Berger had 10.

The Beast powered his 12th circuit blast on June 9, a three-run shot in a 7-6 loss to the Yanks. Gehrig popped No. 12 as well.

Shibe Park was the scene of Jimmie Foxx Day on June 10. XX obtained his 1932 MVP trophy between games of a doubleheader against the Yankees, which Connie Mack's men swept. He showed his appreciation by drill-

ing his 13th home run as Gomez took another pounding. The Babe stayed ahead of the pack, though, banging home runs 13 and 14. But Foxx stayed hot, hitting No. 14 on June 11 in a 13-6 loss to Washington. By June 13, Ruth, Gehrig and Foxx each had 14 homers.

On that day, over in the senior circuit, Klein got five hits in a 15–4 Phils triumph over Brooklyn. On June 29, Hoosier Chuck enjoyed a banner day against the Pirates. A headline could have read: "CHUCK KLEIN 6, PITTSBURGH 4." He went 4-for-4, with home runs 14 and 15, and all six of Philadelphia's RBIs. An article by Stan Baumgartner in the *Philadelphia Inquirer* was headed by the banner, "RUN FOR MAYOR, CHUCK!" and the subhead, "YOU WOULD BE ELECTED EVEN ON THE PROHIBITION TICKET!"

Foxx would have done well on the ballot, too. By the end of June, he was getting hot. In a doubleheader split with the St. Louis Browns on June 30, he went 5-for-5 in the opener, including his 20th four-bagger, two doubles, three runs scored, and three RBIs. Pinky Higgins drove

Jimmie Foxx taking his cuts at Comiskey.

Chuck Klein, in All-Star gear.

were tied at .368. Oddly, Big Jimmie never played in this first classic. Gehrig (.320) started and went all the way, even though the fans, who in a recent series had seen Foxx crush long shots for home runs 16, 17, and 18, were chanting for him throughout the last three innings.

Klein, who went 1-for-4 in right field for the NL, led his league at .369, with 17 homers and 74 RBIs.

The Babe, still in the chase, pumped out three home runs in a doubleheader sweep of the Tigers on July 9. This pushed him up to 22, only two behind Foxx. Klein still led the NL in batting with .368 and in home runs with 17, but Berger was now up to .332 with 15.

For Foxx, No. 26, described as a "cyclopean drive," came on July 15. He also delivered the game-winning hit with the bases loaded in the 11th inning, which aided Grove in triumphing over the Tigers. Klein's bases loaded double helped Snipe Hansen to a victory over the Cards in the second game of a doubleheader on July 16.

While Tennessee repealed prohibition on July 20, Babe Herman swatted three home runs with eight RBIs in a 10-1 Cub crush of the Phillies. Klein went 3-for-4. Herman hit only 16 home runs all year.

Dizzy Dean broke the modern major league strikeout record on July 30, fanning 17 Cubs. This shattered the previous record of 16, jointly held by Noodles Hahn, Christy Mathewson, Rube Waddell, and Nap Rucker. Hubbell pitched two innings of scoreless relief against the Braves to run his consecutive scoreless inning streak —which eventually reached 46—to 40-$\frac{1}{3}$.

Lefty Grove shut out the Yankees on August 3—their first whitewash in 308 games going back to 1931. XX's three-run blast, his 30th homer of the season, clinched the A's victory, and atoned for his being picked off first.

Hoosier Chuck went 4-for-6 and knocked out his 19th four-bagger in a doubleheader with the Giants on August

in six for the A's in the nightcap, also going 5-for-5.

On July 2, the papers were reporting on a probable split between Mary Pickford and Douglas Fairbanks. In Germany, Chancellor Adolf Hitler threatened "ruthless action against his foes." On a happier note, big Double-X had an exceptional day in his continued cannonading against the Brownies. In another split doubleheader, he homered twice in each game, running his total up to 24.

At the All-Star break (the first ever) Foxx's 24 home runs led the AL, while his .366 bating average placed him a close third behind Joe Cronin and Al Simmons, who

5. He was now batting a cool .390.

The man called "The Beast" was again beastly towards the Yankees on August 12, as he popped home runs 33 and 34 in the first game of a doubleheader. No. 33 helped the A's rally to lead 9-6, after they'd trailed 6-0. His 34th, a two-run blast, won the game in the 10th, 11–9.

Rumors began to spread that Klein would be traded to the Cubs for Babe Herman and $100,000. This would have been a real blockbuster, but it didn't come off.

The Beast struck again on August 14 with one of his best days of an already great season. He had four hits, and nine RBIs—four from homer No. 35, a grand slammer. This set an AL one-game RBI record, breaking the old one of eight, held by Roy Hartzell, Joe Jackson, Babe Ruth, Harry Heilmann, Lou Gehrig, Carl Reynolds, Earl Averill...and Jimmie Foxx. XX also hit for the cycle, victimizing Willis Hudlin and Belve Bean in this assault in Cleveland.

His 36th came on August 18. He went 3-for-4 against Detroit, and had three RBIs, raising his league-leading total to 126. He'd pushed his average up to .363, and now led the league by 14 points over former teammate Simmons. Mickey Cochrane went 4-for-4 and was on base for Jimmie's blast. In spite of this, the Tigers topped the A's, 7–6, pushing them to fourth place.

Klein enjoyed a memorable August 19, powering three home runs in a doubleheader sweep of the Reds. He tallied 4-for-9 overall, with two runs scored and six RBIs. Cy Moore pitched his second consecutive shutout. Klein totaled 23 home runs, but Berger passed him for the NL lead on August 23 when he hit his 23rd and 24th.

Foxx went 4-for-5 in a Sunday doubleheader against the White Sox on August 27, with four walks and one run scored. He also displayed his versatility when he got to play shortstop during the second game. With a runner on second for the Sox in the last of the ninth, "acting shortstop Foxx made a splendid stop and blinding throw to retire Dykes for the second out." Foxx also caught and played third during his career, although he's known mainly as a first baseman. He was a great athlete, had reasonable speed for his size, and was considered a good first baseman.

Berger and Klein continued to duel for the NL home run lead, with each blasting their 25th four-bagger on August 31. Klein's 3-for-4, with one run scored and three RBIs, came as the Bucs outslugged the Phils, 13–11.

After a two-week drought, Foxx drilled his 37th home run on September 1. He also tripled, singled and walked twice, with three runs scored and four RBIs. The Senators held an 8-1/2 game lead over the rest of the league,

and Earl Whitehill finally lost after eight consecutive wins. Jimmie led the AL comfortably in batting average at .358 and in home runs with 37. He had 104 runs scored to Gehrig's 113. Klein continued to lead the NL in batting at .381, and was tied with Berger in home runs at 25.

Foxx powered two home runs in a September 2 doubleheader against the Senators, bringing him up to 39. No. 39 was a two-run shot that hit the roof of the left field stands at Shibe. His 40th came on September 5 against the second-place Yankees. In that same game, Gehrig hit No. 23, his first since mid-August.

The Tribe invaded Shibe on September 6, in the battle for third place. Lefty Grove won his 20th, while the Maryland Maestro powered his 41st circuit clout off Mel Harder in the second inning. The ball was blasted into dead center of the big ballpark, and landed on the roof. This gave him his fifth home run in his last five games.

Foxx continued his assault against Tribe pitching when he exploded for his 43rd and 44th home runs on September 9, leading the Mackmen to a sweep of the Indians. After falling to fifth place, the A's were now within one game of third. Foxx's BA now stood at .365.

As Foxx surged, Klein continued in a slump through mid-September. His average was down to .368, but he still led Spud Davis by a comfortable margin. He narrowly led Berger in home runs, and he swatted his 28th and last round tripper of the campaign on September 23, as part of a 6-for-7 doubleheader against the Braves.

Foxx's 48th and final blast came four days later against New York, as he totaled 5 RBIs for the day. His .356 easily outdistanced Manush and Gehrig, and his 163 RBIs put him ahead of all hitters in both leagues. He also scored 125 runs, tallied a .449 on-base percentage, and led in slugging average with .703. If more proof were needed after recent seasons, this was it—Foxx had clearly displaced Ruth as the game's dominant hitter.

On the final day of the season, October 1, Klein and Berger went head-to-head for the home run crown. Berger, who had been out of the lineup for two weeks with the flu, walloped a pinch-hit grand slam to win the game 4–1 and put Boston into fourth place, but Klein still won the title, 28 to 27. Klein easily copped the batting title with a .368 average, compared to Spud Davis at .349, and his 120 RBIs topped the league, too. Hoosier Chuck scored 101 runs and tallied a league-leading 223 hits—his fifth consecutive year of 200 or more hits. He also led the NL with 44 doubles.

The fans of Philadelphia had no pennant to cheer in 1933, but they had something no city has had since—two Triple Crown winners. Will this rarest of events ever happen again? Don't bet on it!

Kid Sisters

Diana Star Helmer

When World War II threatened America and her pastime, factories hired Rosie the Riveter to jump-start U.S. industry, and businessman Philip Wrigley hired Connie "Iron Woman" Wisniewski to keep baseball alive.

Wrigley, manufacturer and Chicago Cubs owner, began planning the All American Girls Professional Baseball League only weeks after war was declared. By 1943, Racine and Kenosha, Wisconsin, Rockford, Illinois and South Bend, Indiana were ready to take the field with a hybrid game. Girls ball took advantage of players' existing softball skills while accelerating action for spectator appeal. Local business sponsors and not-for-profit status gave All Americans additional impetus, as proceeds went to community good-will.

The number of teams had doubled by 1946, with franchises in Muskegon and Grand Rapids, Michigan, Fort Wayne, Indiana and Peoria, Illinois. Attendance grew too, from 176,612 in 1943 to 754,919 in 1946, the year side-arm pitching, longer basepaths and a smaller, 11-inch ball were introduced.

Fans poured in and the talent pool shriveled as the game grew away from softball. So when the Muskegon Lassies yearbook printed a little girl's wish to "be a Lassie when I grow up," team sponsors wondered: why wait 'til she's grown?

If girls started playing ball sooner, there would be more and better pros to recruit later. Junior Teams would be a perfect community service project for the non-profit All-Americans and other organizations that wanted to "fight juvenile delinquency." Interest and

need were demonstrated when Kiwanis-sponsored "Knothole Gangs" yielded hundreds of children signing up for free games.

The first All-American "juniors" team, the South Bend Bobbie Soxers (after the South Bend Blue Sox), debuted in 1946. The Racine Belles, Kenosha Comets, Rockford Peaches, Fort Wayne Daisies and Muskegon Lassies followed soon after They all called their youth teams simply Juniors.

In 1947 Racine, four new Junior Belles teams were named for their uniform colors. The Reds, Grays, Golds and Greens wore skirted suits stylistically identical to the "big Belles." A local store donated the fabric. Racine women sewed the uniforms. Players would bring their own shoes and gloves, with the big Belles donating other equipment and umpire fees.

More than 100 girls came to a Racine park for preliminary training sessions. Tryouts would be two weeks later, after coaches knew the kids, knew how quickly they learned and how hard they were willing to try.

"Some of them were so uncoordinated at first, they couldn't break a pane of glass," Junior Belles coach Herb Hoppe said of those early days. Yet, after a lifetime of semipro ball, Hoppe couldn't help liking these little girls who "wanted to practice every day."

Janet Wells was such a girl. Yet she scarcely believed it when her strict father read to her from the paper about Junior Belles training. "Papa, may I really?" she asked. Years later, she imitated his growling reply, "Playing ball is good for you. Go."

"We played like little toughies," Janet remembered. But after every inning, she would take out a comb and straighten her long, black curls.

Diana Star Helmer is the author of Belles of the Ballpark *(Millbrook Press), from which this article is adapted.*

The coaches assigned 15 girls to each team. The youngest was 12; the oldest, 14. After players were assigned, coaches drew straws for groups, just as senior circuit coaches did. In subsequent years, the Junior Belles had no formal tryouts. Coaches and prospects bargained individually, but teams couldn't carry too many people, because every Junior played in every game.

It was hard for Hoppe to turn anyone away. He had kids of his own, and knew there weren't many other activities for them in 1947 Racine. No wonder kids wanted to practice every day. No wonder no one ever missed a practice or a game. Hoppe came home from work each day to find his neighbor girl in the drive, waiting to play catch. "We compromised and practiced three or four times a week," he said. Hoppe, like the other coaches, volunteered his time. Umpires were paid for the intramural competitions on Saturdays and Tuesdays, but they were local, so if parents objected to a call, they did so politely.

Janet Wells remembered, "It was the honor of my life to be chosen." Her family understood. When a big wedding came up on the day of a game, Janet was taken to both. "There I am in the old pictures. Everyone is in gowns, and I'm in my pantalettes and short dress. Everybody kept saying how cute my uniform was."

Such dedication paid off. "I took a lot of time with them," Hoppe said, "and after a while, they became good players. They learned to run and catch and slide. They learned to throw overhand, even curves." If someone told Janet she "threw like a boy," she considered that a compliment.

"They played hard," Hoppe said. "There was no fooling around."

Juniors games were held in city parks, with all four teams competing at once. The Wells family walked from one game to the other, because Janet and her sister were on different teams. Employees of "big" Belles sponsors attended games to see friends and to please their bosses. Coach Hoppe worked for Western Publishing, a Belles benefactor. He saw almost everyone from work at Juniors games, sometimes 300 people.

But Janet remembers best the occasional Juniors game at Horlick Field just before a real Belles game. "That was like being in heaven," she said. Afterwards, Juniors could attend the grown-up games for free, as they could any time they wore their caps to the ballpark. On rare occasions, Juniors teams traveled with the seniors. In 1952, the Junior Daisies and South Bend Bobbie Soxers took the field in Fort Wayne prior to a game by their "big sisters."

Local newspapers took Junior league baseball as seriously as adult play. Junior tryouts, team rosters and even uniforms were reported with the same enthusiasm given the older girls.

Hoppe remembered being able to ask his employer for anything the team needed, even missing an hour of work to attend to team matters. Employers were glad to have workers contribute to the community, and gave people like Hoppe the freedom to do so. "Times were different," Hoppe would say years later. "There wasn't as much stress. There was no one telling me to do this or that with my team. And I got to know some of the girls, some of the parents. You could feel you were doing something. You could feel the kids appreciated it."

Times were different in many ways. In 1947, 14-year-old girls were considered too young for boy friends. They did have friends who were boys, and Hoppe remembered that boys often came to Juniors games, throwing warm-ups with the players they knew.

"One boy came to every game and hid behind a tree," Janet said. "He'd always ask me if I wanted to get a soda, and I always told him no."

Between work and Junior Belles ball, Hoppe "never had a day to myself." He made his 8-year-old daughter a batgirl so he could see her more often, and hoped that someday she would be a Junior Belle.

But by 1950, the Belles, like other All-American teams, were beginning to struggle. The stress-free times Hoppe spoke of were changing, and Girls Baseball was a product of those times.

The All American ball shrank more, trying to convince the public that Girls Ball was as action-packed as men's. Pitches went to overhand, with longer basepaths. Yet the Racine Belles, after helping support other AAGPBL teams that resisted centralized management, went in the red once too often. Their last season was 1950.

All American teams folded and relocated until 1954, the last season for Girls Baseball and most of its Junior teams. Only the Fort Wayne Daisies Juniors lit the summers until 1963, playing with the rules and skirted uniforms of the AAGPBL.

Other cities forgot the All Americans. In 1954, the Racine Journal Times wrote about the new youth activity called Little League. Though Girls Baseball had recently been a part of Racine, no one asked why girls weren't allowed to play, or why newspapers wrote of fathers who would coach while mothers would simply "cheer."

Twenty years later, in 1974, another Racine news brief told of plans to start a softball league for fifth and sixth grade girls. Twice the writer mentioned that girls were "enthusiastic but inexperienced." Racine, like other towns, had long assumed girls would have no interest in athletics.

Ten years later still, in 1984, a 13-year-old Racine girl had to fight for the chance to pitch for the Racine County Youth Sports Association. A news article stated that it took an entire year for the coach and her teammates—all boys—to grant her respect as a player, not as a girl.

The history of the All American was forgotten, and has finally started its repeat. Maybe the news from 1994 will be better.

Field of Dreams

Gene Carney

Yeah, guess I'm a member of AA:
Alienated by Astroturf
Hey, most of us never played on plastic
Grass is the missing link
Between all the games of our lives—
Sandlot, Little League, school—
And theirs

But why stop at replanting the real green?
Why not make the playing fields
Even more connecting?

Let's plant trees around the outfield
Let the warning track burst into colors
For the Series

Let the outfielders fish around in thorny bramble
For lost balls in the gaps
(Both sides hunt til it's found)

Let the thieves slide into flat rocks
That don't give anything but bruises

Let glass windows be
Strategically placed
Near the bullpens, maybe
Batters breaking them get the bases
But it costs them ten thou each
(The fines go to charity)

Let the field of our dreams
Have its cornfield in right center
Ground rule double in the stalks
Let vendors sell the cobs: "Souven-*ears* here!"

Let the infield undulate some
With a sprinkling of pebbles
To keep those wizards on their toes

Let all fielders wear gloves
Without all that trapping and padding
So their hands sting some—
The price of earned POs and As

Let them keep the ball in play
As in the days before the Babe
Til they knock the covers off
Keep tape handy for extra innings
Now there's a game worth the price of admission

Gene Carney , of Utica, NY, is the author of Romancing the Horsehide:
Baseball Poems on Players and the Game, *published by McFarland
this past spring, from which this poem is taken.*